SOCIAL MORALITY
IN ISLAM

SOCIAL MORALITY IN ISLAM

An Introductory Guide for Young Readers

Asım Şark

NEW JERSEY • LONDON • FRANKFURT • CAIRO

TUGHRA
BOOKS
New Jersey

Published by Tughra Books
335 Clifton Avenue, Clifton
New Jersey 07011, USA

www.tughrabooks.com

Library of Congress Cataloging-in-Publication Data
Sark, Asim.
[Güzel ahlak sahibi olmak. English]
Social morality in Islam : an introductory guide for young readers / Asim Sark ; translated by Erhan Yükselci.
pages cm
ISBN 978-1-59784-344-7 (alk. paper)
1. Islamic ethics. 2. Islam--Social aspects. 3. Muslim youth--Conduct of life. I. Title.
BJ1292.Y6S2713 2015
297.5--dc23
2015022876

ISBN: 978-1-59784-344-7

Translated by Erhan Yükselci

Printed by
Imak Ofset, Istanbul - Turkey

Contents

1.

WHY ARE GOOD MANNERS
SO IMPORTANT?

"The best inheritance a parent leaves their children is good manners."[1]

Why Good Manners?

There is no other religion or system that gives as much importance to good manners as Islam. The noble Prophet, peace and blessings be upon him, said, "Islam is good manners." Having good manners is the greatest sign of being a Muslim. There are many *hadith*s (traditions) of the blessed Prophet encouraging good conduct. For example, "The most perfect in his faith among the believers is the one who has good manners." The beloved Prophet, who emphasized the importance of good conduct over faith, conveys the means becoming close to him in the following *hadith*: "On the Day of Judgment the dearest and closest to me, as regard of my company, are those who bear the best moral character."

In the Holy Qur'an, there are many verses encouraging good manners such as keeping one's promises, forgiveness, humbleness, obeying parents, trustfulness, affection, brotherliness, peace, sincerity, generosity, compassion, tolerance, speaking with kindness, being good humored, and purity of heart.

In addition, there are also many verses of the Qur'an regarding avoiding bad manners and conduct such as oppression, ostentation, abusive-

---

[1] *Sunan at-Tirmidhi*, Birr, 33.

ness, greed, selfishness, jealousy, pride, animosity, suspicion, waste and mischief-making, which also signifies the importance the Islamic faith gives to good manners and conduct.

So why should we be well mannered? We can address this topic in a few paragraphs:

1. In addition to worship, the Islamic faith gives great importance particularly to social relations, and it is impossible for those who do not have good morals to live their religion to perfection.

2. Prophet Muhammad, peace and blessings be upon him, represented good manners. In order to become an inhabitant of Paradise, it is necessary to be adorned with his good morals. In the Qur'an, Allah conveys that the noble Prophet is the most excellent example for every believer. In another verse the Qur'an reveals, *"You are surely of a sublime character"* (al-Qalam 68:4). The only way a person can live like the Messenger of Allah is by emulating his excellent morals and conduct.

3. When a believer has good morals, he can be elevated to the level of those who are absorbed in worship. The noble Prophet defined this in one of the traditions in these words: "By his good character, a believer will attain the degree of one who prays during the night and fasts during the day." This should not be misinterpreted. Worship is extremely important in terms of displaying servitude to Allah. But in addition, a believer who lives in a society must comply with the conduct necessary in relationships between people within that society. When he achieves this, or in other words, when he is a person of good manners and conduct, then his worship would have reached perfection.

4. Having good morals is the means by which a believer may enter Paradise. When a man asked the noble Prophet which act would lead the people into entering Paradise the most, he replied, "Piety and fine morals," which signifies the importance of good manners together with worship.

5. Good manners signify perfection and maturity in religion and faith. The noble Prophet identified two characteristics not found

in a believer—greed and bad manners. Again, he affirmed that the best among believers regarding faith were those of good manners.

6. Good manners and conduct are also forms of servitude to Allah. In other words, having good manners is a form of worship. Indeed, the noble Prophet stated that the simplest forms of worship are refraining from speaking unnecessarily and good conduct.

7. Displaying good manners is a sign of love for Allah and His Messenger. This is clearly defined in the tradition stating that those closest to the Messenger of Allah on the Day of Judgment will be those of good conduct. When Allah loves His servant, He grants him good manners.

8. Good manners eliminate sin in the same way that the sun eliminates frost: good manners melt away sin as water melts ice. The noble Prophet explained that bad manners spoil a good deed just as vinegar spoils honey. Therefore, we should all recite this supplication of the noble Prophet: "O Lord! I ask You for health, restraint, trustworthiness, good character and contentment with the decree. O most Compassionate! I ask You to grant this by virtue of Your compassion."

Allah's Messenger: The Paragon of Grace

Allah's Messenger displayed a profound example of grace in response to the offensive, coarse and derisive words and actions of those around him, approaching his addressees with tenderness. Nobody in the presence of Allah's Messenger sensed even the slightest coarse or belittling attitude to come from him. Offending and hurtful words never fell from his lips. He never uttered insulting or defamatory statements even if implicitly.

Stating, "The best of you is the best of you in character," Allah's Messenger stressed that a person's grace and kindness towards their friends is an act of goodness and that every act of goodness is a charity. He once gave his Companions the glad tidings of lofty palaces in Paradise the inside of which could be seen from the outside and the outside of which could be seen from the inside. When a Bedouin hearing this asked who these buildings would be for, Allah's Messenger said that these were for courteous people and for those who were soft spoken.

Our mother Aisha, may Allah be pleased with her, narrated: "One day, the Messenger of Allah came to my room, turned to the qibla, opened up his hands, and prayed: 'My Lord! I am only a human being. Please do not punish me if I had offended one of Your servants.'"[2]

Anas ibn Malik, who spent long years in the service of the blessed Prophet, reported that Allah's Messenger had the best disposition amongst people: "He sent me on an errand one day, and I said: 'By Allah, I would not go.' I had, however, this idea in my mind that I would do as Allah's Messenger had commanded me to do. I went out until I happened to come across children who had been playing in the street. In the meanwhile, Allah's Messenger came there and he caught me by the back of my neck from behind me. As I looked towards him I found him smiling and he said: Unays, did you go where I commanded you to go?' I said: 'O Allah's Messenger, yes, I am going.' Anas further said: 'I served him for nine years but I know not that he ever said to me about a thing which I had done why I did that, or about a thing I had left as to why I had not done that.'"[3]

He Refrained from Idle Conversation

Allah's Messenger was constantly of genial, good-natured and tender-hearted. He was not coarse or hardhearted. He would not scream and shout, speak ill in any way, or criticize others. He would overlook those things that displeased him. Those appealing to him would not be disappointed. He forbade himself three things: Debate, exaggeration and futile talk. He severed connection with the people in the following three aspects: He would condemn no one, would not pry into the faults of others, and would not say anything apart from that of which he was hopeful of reward. Those listening to him when he spoke would bow their heads forward, as though birds were perched upon their heads, and

---

2   Ahmad ibn Hanbal, *Al-Musnad*, 6/180.
3   *Sahih Muslim*, Book 43, Hadith 74.

were attentive to the utmost. When he spoke, those in the assembly would fall silent and the people would speak when he fell silent.

There would be no dispute or quarrel in the presence of Allah's Messenger. He would smile at what his Companions smiled at and marvel at what they marveled at. When a stranger was coarse in their speech or request, he would show patience.

When his Companions chided such a stranger, he said to them, "When you see a person seeking an object earnestly, assist him in obtaining his need."

The Prophet Would Meet the Needs of Destitute Ones

We all know Bilal as the muezzin (caller to Prayer) for the Messenger of Allah, peace and blessings be upon him. But Bilal had another duty, entrusted to him by the blessed Prophet: to attend to the visitors. When the Prophet saw that a Muslim was in desperate straits, he would summon Bilal and tell him to provide food and clothes for that Muslim. If there was no food or clothes to provide to that Muslim, Bilal would borrow money to satisfy his needs. That money would later be repaid.

Once a group of Emigrants wearing a simple dress had come barefoot to visit the Prophet. Seeing their state, the Messenger of Allah became upset and he told Bilal to recite the call to Prayer. When Muslims came to the mosque in response to the call to Prayer, the Prophet called on them to help these Emigrants. The Companions heeded his call and quickly collected money to buy decent clothing to them.

He Was Someone from among People Who Was Always Close to People

The Messenger of Allah would be in remembrance of Allah as he sat down or stood up. He wouldn't set a special place or post for himself to sit. He would forbid people from searching for a special place to sit in social gatherings. When he went to a social gathering, he would sit down in any available place and urged people to act in the same way.

He would show close interest in everyone sitting in his presence. But no one would think he was held in higher esteem than others. When he was sitting or standing together with someone, he wouldn't be the first to leave the gathering, even for any need. When people conveyed their needs to him, he would either accept their requests or give them proper advice with gentle words.

Thanks to his tolerance and good character, people would seek refuge in him; they saw him as their father. Everyone had equal rights before him. Being in his close company, people would feel mildness, modesty, and forbearance. When he was around, no one would raise his voice or humiliate other people or talk about other people's mistakes. People would be treated equally as they believed that only criterion for superiority is one's God-fearing quality (*taqwa*). His Companions were humble people. They would show respect to the elderly and treat kids with love. They would help the needy people with an altruistic urge and they would protect foreigners.[4]

READING TEXT
Youth

Those who wish to predict a nation's future can do so accurately by analyzing the education and upbringing given to its young people.

* * *

Desires resemble sweets, and virtues resemble food that is a little salty or sour. When young people are free to choose, what are they likely to prefer? So, it is our obligation to bring them up to be friends of virtue and enemies of indecency and immorality.

* * *

Until we help our young people through education, they are captives of their environment, lusts, and pleasures. They wander about aimlessly, moved by intense passions and far away from knowledge and reason. They can become truly valiant young representatives of the na-

---

4   *Zaman*, Ailem weekly, No 174, pp. 17–20.

tional thought and feeling only if their education integrates them with their past and prepares them intelligently for their future.

* * *

Think of society as a crystal vessel, and of its young people as the liquid poured into it. Notice that the liquid assumes the vessel's shape and color. Evil-minded champions of regimentation tell young people to obey them instead of the truth. Do such people never question themselves? Should they not also obey the truth?

* * *

A nation's progress or decline depends on the spirit and consciousness, the upbringing and education, given to its young people. Nations that have raised their young people correctly are always ready for progress, while those who have not done so find it impossible to take even a single step forward.

* * *

Little attention and importance is given to teaching cultural values, although they are essential to education. When we give them their deserved importance, we will have reached a major objective.

* * *

Young people are saplings of power, strength, and intelligence. If trained and educated properly, they can become "heroes" overcoming obstacles and acquire a mind that promises enlightenment to hearts and order to the world.[5]

QUESTIONS

1. What is the best heritage parents may leave behind for their children?

   a. House   b. Car

   c. Fine morals   d. Money

2. In which respect did our Prophet describe believers with fine morals as the most mature believers?

   a. In terms of worship   b. In terms of belief

---

[5] Gülen, M. Fethullah, *Pearls of Wisdom*, New Jersey: Tughra Books, 2012, pp. 39; 44–45.

    c. In terms of family life   d. In terms of social life

3. Which of the following phrases best fits the blanks in the *hadith*, "With the help of ...., one can attain the degree of a person who says Prayers all through the night and fasts in the scorching heat?"

    a. Fine morals   b. Parents

    c. Friends   d. Self-confidence

4. Which of the following were the two deeds our Prophet stated in response to a person who asked him about the deeds which are most likely to make people worthy of Paradise?

    a. Piety and fine morals   b. Silence and contemplation

    c. Reading and supplication   d. Working and excellence

5. Who was the distinguished Companion, known as the "Prophet's Attendant" for serving the Prophet for 9 years during which the noble Prophet didn't chide him in the slightest manner?

    a. Abdullah ibn Mas'ud   b. Ali

    c. Zayd ibn Haritha   d. Anas ibn Malik

6. Who was the distinguished Companion who was not only the muezzin (caller to Prayer) for the Prophet, but also would take care of his visitors?

    a. Anas ibn Malik   b. Zayd ibn Haritha

    c. Bilal al-Habashi   d. Abu Mahzura

7. Which phrase best fills in the blank in the sentence, "Little attention and importance is given to teaching ...., although they are essential to education."?

    a. Quantitative courses   b. Foreign language courses

    c. Verbal courses   d. Cultural values

8. What is usually the reason for impertinence in children?

    a. Lack of proper thinking/reasoning practices in the family

    b. Foggy quality of the sources for their education

    c. Chaotic nature of feelings and actions in the family

    d. All of the above

2.

RIGHTS OF PARENTS

"The contentment of the father—or the mother, in another narration—is the door to Paradise. It is up to you to keep or lose this door."[6]

Rights of Parents

Our parents play a vital role in our coming into the world and they are certainly the source of life under the principle of cause and effect. Man is weak and helpless upon birth, but with Allah's grace, he steps into a world full of vast clemency and compassion from his parents. Until he attains a certain age, his parents sacrificially do everything for him. They even give up their basic needs such as nutrition and clothing in order to make sure their child is properly fed and clothed. They face all sorts of difficulties for their child. Our parents are our first guides.

Showing respect to parents is a primary and sacred obligation. Islam attaches great importance to parents. Like many values that are lost to oblivion, the respect for parents is forgotten as well. Although we are highly indebted to them, we may start to perceive our parents as a burden.

However, our Lord attaches great importance to parents. It would be a great misfortune for children not to show earnest respect to parents who are esteemed by Allah. Let us elaborate on this matter with the following verses from the Holy Qur'an:

---

6   *Sunan at-Tirmidhi*, Birr, 3; Ahmad ibn Hanbal, *Al-Musnad*, 5/197.

> Your Lord has decreed that you worship none but Him alone, and
> treat parents with the best of kinds. Should one of them, or both,
> attain old age in your lifetime, do not say 'Ugh!' to them (as an indi-
> cation of complaint or impatience), nor push them away; and always
> address them in gracious words. Lower to them the wing of humil-
> ity out of mercy, and say: 'My Lord, have mercy on them even as
> they cared for me in childhood. (Al-Isra 17:23–24).

In these verses, Allah asks His servants to treat their parents with
kindness and tenderness. Here, Allah chooses to mention the kindness
to parents immediately after stressing the importance of worshiping
Allah and even without referring to significance of belief in Prophets.
In order to avoid any confusion, the verses stress the importance of worshiping Allah alone before placing emphasis on the significance of treating parents with "kindness" (*ihsan*). Thus, worship is to Allah and kindness is to parents.

The verses also draw attention to how we should treat our parents
when they grow old. Here, one can wonder about the wise purpose
behind this emphasis on the form of treatment that should be afforded
to parents in their old age. The verses first assert that kindness to parents is important at all times. Then, they move on to note that people
should show added kindness and benevolence to parents as they grow
old. This is because our parents will become more emotional and may
start to nurture certain expectations from us in their old ages. At that
time, they deserve to be treated with kindness as Allah is entitled to be
worshiped alone.

When one of the spouses who spent their lifetime together for 40
or 50 years dies, the surviving spouse suffers from a serious trauma. Many
people who spent their lives in peace and happiness are seen crying next
to the graves of their dead spouses. Thus, when one spouse dies, it
becomes the duty of their children to fill the gap left by the departing
spouse. This gap cannot be filled by taking the surviving parent to nursing home where he or she can be treated perfectly. A nursing home may
even prove to be torturous for him/her. Indeed, the old age and approaching death—which calls attention to itself with the deaths of the spouse,
close relatives and friends—create a persistent sense of great loneliness.

This solitude can be dispelled away only by his/her children. For this reason, the Holy Qur'an dictates that we should treat our parents with added kindness when one or both grow old.

It is interesting to note that the Qur'an uses the phrase "ihsan" to describe kind treatment of parents. This phrase also means "worshiping Allah as if you see Him." By implication, we can say that when they treat their parents with kinds, people should act as if they see Allah. One or both parents may become dependent on the patronage of their children. As they grow old, parents may comfort each other for a certain time, but they may not be able to work and perform self-care. In some cases, one has to take care of both parents. This may mean added costs and responsibilities for the child who takes care of his/her parents. But people who take care of their surviving parents may have to deal also with the potential trauma surviving parents may feel in connection with their spouses who die.

In such cases, the Qur'an emphatically enjoins us not to say "Ugh!" to them. By prohibiting the slightest sign of impatience, Allah prevents us from engaging in graver forms of disrespect toward our parents. As a matter of fact, when a person says nothing, but only "Ugh" in the face of a positive suggestion by his/her parents, this may sound to them like the end of the world. Given the fact that we are forbidden even from saying "Ugh" to our parents, we cannot beat them or revile at them or send them packing to nursing homes. Rather, we must take care of them in the best way possible and please them in their old age when they need affection and love the most from us.

In the latter part of the verse, with added emphasis, Allah prescribes us not to "push them away" and not to speak harsh words to them.

"Always address them in gracious words," the Holy Qur'an urges believers in the verse, teaching them how to treat their parents, especially when they are old.

"*Lower to them the wing of humility out of mercy,*" the Qur'an further advises pronouncedly, adding: "*And say: 'My Lord, have mercy on them even as they cared for me in childhood.'*" Indeed, Prophet Abraham, upon him be peace, prayed to Allah, saying: "*Our Lord! Forgive me, and my parents, and all the believers, on the Day on which the Reckoning will be established"* (Ibrahim 14:41).

In the verse, the phrase, "as they cared for me in childhood," in the verse draws attention to our state when we are first born to this world as well as to how our parents go through various hardships and make certain sacrifices and reprogram their lives in taking care of us, making us realize that we should treat them with similar sensibility as a show of our thankfulness to them.

Never Show Impatience or Anger to Your Parents

> Should one of them, or both, attain old age in your lifetime, do not say "ugh!" to them (as an indication of complaint or impatience), nor push them away. (Al-Isra 17:23).

In this verse of the Qur'an, Allah is guiding people regarding how they should address and behave towards their parents. An offspring is not even permitted to utter "ugh" in complaint—let alone insult—towards parents, nor allowed to become upset or raise a hand to parents in anger. The Qur'an defined the boundaries of disrespect to parents. While saying "ugh" in complaint towards a parent has been prohibited, how can we possibly display acts of disrespect, abuse and offensive behavior? In these terms, using any word classified as offensive as—or more offensive than—"ugh" is disrespectful, and means disobedience towards parents. Respect towards parents is a very important and delicate issue, and by no means should this topic ever be underemphasized. If this was not a matter of such importance, Allah would not have placed such emphasis on the subject and depicted such delicate boundaries regarding respect towards parents. In terms of respect and obedience to parents, not only those distant from religious and civil manners but sometimes those who believe they strive for the sake of religion and the nation can also make grave mistakes. Whereas while a person is occupied with acts that please Allah on one hand, on the other hand they should not destroy their good deeds in this world by doing things that displease Allah.

Gratitude towards the Creator and then towards One's Parents

Allah the Almighty declares in the Qur'an: "*We have enjoined on human in respect with his parents: his mother bore him in strain upon strain, and his weaning was in two years. (So, O human,) be thankful to Me and to your parents. To Me is the final homecoming*" (Luqman 31:14).

Our Lord conveys the following message to us by means of this verse: Just as We once entrusted the child to its mother and father, We have now entrusted the mother and father to the child and have advised them to approach them with kindness, as when their mother carried them, she bore countless difficulties such as pain and suffering during pregnancy and a close brush with death during birth. After giving birth to them, she then breastfed them for two years in order for them to rise to their feet. It is for this reason that you have been enjoined to show gratitude first to Allah, Who created you, and then to your parents who served as the agency in this creation.

It deserves notice that Allah renders the mother and father partner in the thanks that needs to be shown to Him and reveals that they share the very same right with Him. This is because a person who displays thankfulness to their parents in the perfect sense is also ready to expand with thanks towards Allah. Contrary to this, it cannot be said that a person who completely disregards them and waits for their death has any real connection with Allah. At the end of the verse, Allah says, "To Me is the final homecoming." In other words, this statement says, so to speak: As you have bowed at the feet of others despite being created by and having received your sustenance from Me, and due to your scorning your parents and abandoning them to their own resources despite their having raised and cared for you, I will call you to account at the Great Reckoning.

In the verse immediately following, a different facet of obedience to one's parents is indicated thus: "But if they strive with you to make you associate with Me something of which you certainly have no knowledge (and which is absolutely contrary to the Knowledge), do not obey them. Even then, treat them with kindness and due consideration in respect of (the life of) this world. Follow the way of him who has turned to Me with utmost sincerity and committed himself to seeking My approval. Then, (O all human beings,) to Me is your return, and then I will make you understand all that you were doing (and call you to account)."

If they compel you to associate partners with Allah due to their ignorance, then do not obey them in this regard, as Allah's rights take precedence over everything else. But even if they be polytheists, you are not to fail in doing good to them, treating them well, and in pursuing your necessary struggle in the way of Allah in such a manner.

The following Prophetic Tradition narrated by Abu Bakr, may Allah be pleased with him, offers yet another dimension to the matter: The Messenger of Allah, upon him be peace and blessings, said, "Shall I not inform you of the greatest of the major sins?" and he repeated this thrice. When we said, "Yes O Messenger of Allah," he said: "Associating partners with Allah, disobedience to parents, and taking a life."

At that time Allah's Messenger was leaning against something and he sat up and said, "And telling lies and giving false testimony." And He kept repeating these so many times that we said, "If only he would be quiet."

It is noteworthy that in this Prophetic Tradition, disobedience to one's parents is considered in the same way as the major sins of associating partners with Allah, killing, lying and bearing false testimony. Consequently, here, the rights of parents, the rights of Allah, the rights of the individual and the society are considered within the same category.

As a final point, the following incident which took place in the Age of Happiness, vividly demonstrates the importance of observing the rights of parents:

A person came to the Messenger of Allah and informed him of a young man who was on his deathbed but was unable to recite the Declaration of Faith despite being urged to do so. Allah's Messenger asked, "Did this man offer his Prayers?" Upon receiving an answer in the affirmative, he immediately got up and went straight to the house of the dying man along with those next to him. Allah's Messenger approached the young man and instructed him to say the words, "There is no deity but Allah." When the young man indicated that he was unable to do so, Allah's Messenger sensed the possibility of offense between this man and his mother and then sent for the mother of the dying man. When his elderly mother arrived, the Prophet asked her whether any discontentment existed between them.

Crying, the woman said that her son constantly hurt her and that she harbored a disappointment towards him that she was unable to overcome. Allah's Messenger then said to the woman, "If were to light a fire here and say to you, 'If you forgive your son, we will release him, otherwise, we will throw him into this fire,' would you forgive him?"

The noble Prophet's words, "Otherwise we will throw him into this fire," melted away any disappointment the woman felt towards her son and she took Allah and His Messenger as her witness that she was pleased with her son.

Then turning to the young man, Allah's Messenger instructed him to declare, "There is no deity but Allah. He is One. He has no partners and Muhammad is His servant and His Messenger."

Just as soon as the Prophet completed his words, the young man found the words flowing out of his mouth. Seeing and being considerably pleased by this, Allah's Messenger smiled and said, "All praise be to Allah, Who saved this man from the flames of the Fire through me."

Hence, observing the rights of parents, which are trampled in our day, to the exalted degree attached to them in Islam and striving to earn the pleasure and approval of parents while they are still alive is the duty of every child.

Sa'id ibn Abi Burda relates an incident that his father heard from Ibn Umar. One day, Ibn Umar saw a Yamani man circumambulating the Ka'ba while carrying his mother on his back, saying, "I am your humble camel..." Catching sight of Ibn Umar, he asked him, "Ibn Umar, do you think that I have repaid her?" Ibn Umar replied, "No, not even for a single contraction."

A man once came to Umar, who was famed for his justice, and asked, "I have an old mother who is unable to see to her own needs, so I carry her on my back. I also help her in performing the ablution. Whilst doing all this, I never once made her feel indebted or obliged. Have I fulfilled my duty towards her?"

"No," Umar answered. The man demonstrated his astonishment saying, "Even though I rendered my back her mount and devoted myself to her?"

Umar made this striking observation in response: "Your mother too used to do the same for you (when you were young) in the hope that you would live long. As for you—in serving her, you wait for when she will go away (die)."

Abu Nawfal narrates: "One day a man approached Umar and said that he had committed murder. Umar asked him whether he had done so intentionally or by accident.

When the man responded that he had done so accidentally, Umar asked him whether his parents were still alive. The man said that his father was still living and Umar gave him the following counsel: "Go to your father without delay and be of service to him. Do whatever you can to please him."

Umar then added, "I swear by Allah that were his mother still alive and had he been of service to her, I could have been hopeful that the Fire would not engulf this man for all eternity."

Kindness to parents functions as the Divine steed Buraq taking the human being to Paradise. Earning Paradise and reaching it with ease is contingent upon being a believer and earning the pleasure of one's parents. That is to say, if they are not pleased with us, we are face to face with the threat of not being amongst the first people to enter Paradise, as earning their approval amounts to earning Allah's approval. Breaking their hearts amounts to disobliging Allah. Those who behave in this way will not be able to attain the bliss of being among the first to enter Paradise. According to a narration reported by Aisha, the Messenger of Allah saw himself enter Paradise in a dream and heard someone reciting the Qur'an. Upon Allah's Messenger asking, "Who is reciting?" it was said to him, "Haritha ibn al-Nu'man."

Of the Helpers, the natives of Medina, this Companion participated in all the battles including Badr, Uhud, and the Battle of the Trench. He is one of the shining examples of virtue among the Companions.

Despite all these elevated characteristics, the Prophet explained the reason for this Companion's entry into Paradise as follows:

"Such is the reward of kindness (towards one's parents)." After thrice repeating this statement, Allah's Messenger added, "Haritha ibn Nu'man was most kind and reverent to his mother."

Such is the exemplary lesson for us all from Allah's Messenger, as to where one of the keys to Paradise is to be found. If we wish to attain the Paradise we have lost, we must take our parents by the hand and treat them with utmost kindness, compassion and respect, so that they can pull us along with them to Paradise.

The Prayers of Those Who Please Their Parents Are Acceptable

Ibn Umar narrated: "The Messenger of Allah said, 'While three persons were walking, rain began to fall and they had to enter a cave in a mountain. A big rock rolled over and blocked the mouth of the cave. They said to each other, 'Invoke Allah with the best deed you have performed (so Allah might remove the rock)'. One of them said, 'O Allah! My parents were old and I used to go out for grazing (my animals). On my return I would milk (the animals) and take the milk in a vessel to my parents to drink. After they had drunk from it, I would give it to my children, family and wife. One day I was delayed and on my return I found my parents sleeping, and I disliked to wake them up. The children were crying at my feet (because of hunger). That state of affairs continued till it was dawn. O Allah! If You regard that I did it for Your sake, then please remove this rock so that we may see the sky.' So, the rock was moved a bit. The second said, 'O Allah! You know that I was in love with a cousin of mine, like the deepest love a man may have for a woman, and she told me that I would not get my desire fulfilled unless I paid her one-hundred Dinars (gold pieces). So, I struggled for it till I gathered the desired amount, and when I sat in between her legs, she told me to be afraid of Allah, and asked me not to deflower her except rightfully (by marriage). So, I got up and left her. O Allah! If You regard that I did it for Your sake, kindly remove this rock.' So, two-thirds of the rock was removed. Then the third man said, 'O Allah!

No doubt You know that once I employed a worker for one *Faraq* (three *Sa*'s) of *millet*, and when I wanted to pay him, he refused to take it, so I sowed it and from its yield I bought cows and a shepherd. After a time that man came and demanded his money. I said to him: Go to those cows and the shepherd and take them for they are for you. He asked me whether I was joking with him. I told him that I was not joking with him, and all that belonged to him. O Allah! If You regard that I did it sincerely for Your sake, then please remove the rock.' So, the rock was removed completely from the mouth of the cave."

As can be seen in the Prophetic Tradition, three helpless people entreated Allah by making their sincere deeds intercede on their behalf and Allah opened the door of deliverance to them. The actions of each are most superior and virtuous. In particular, if we are to consider the example concerning the subject in question, we see that serving one's parents and pleasing them opens a door of mystery at times where the human being is most in difficulty. Allah accepted the prayer of a person who did not fail in service to their parents and who preferred them to their own children, and thus delivered them from the cave.

What Allah's Messenger Enjoins about the Rights of Parents

The following Prophetic Traditions are most meaningful with respect to their demonstrating the sensitivity of Allah's Messenger in the matter of the rights of parents:

A Companion came to Allah's Messenger requesting permission to partake in jihad. The Prophet asked (despite knowing the response), "Are your parents alive?" When the Companion replied, "Yes," he said, "Then exert yourself on their behalf (in service to them)."

The Messenger of Allah was aware that that Companion's parents were alive and in need of care. That Companion wanted to perform jihad in the path of exalting and communicating the Divine Name and message.

There was, however, the possibility of being killed or wounded on the battlefield. Jihad is a great ideal aimed at striving to exalt the Name of Allah, an ideal of which there is no greater.

To those once asking, "O Allah's Messenger, which deed is equal to jihad undertaken in the path of Allah?" he replied, "You do not have the strength to do it."

The question was repeated twice or even thrice, but each time he answered, "You do not have the strength to undertake it." Then he said, "One who goes out for jihad (*mujahid*) in Allah's cause is like a person who observes the fast, stands in Prayer constantly, recites and obeys the verses of the Qur'an and does not exhibit any laxity in fasting and Prayer until the one undertaking jihad in Allah's way returns."

Whilst embarking upon precisely such a struggle for which there is no equivalent, the Messenger of Allah, taking into consideration the sorrowful situation of his indigent parents, instructed the individual seeking permission to participate in jihad to, "Exert yourself on their behalf (in service to them)."

In another narration in Muslim a Companion said, "I pledge allegiance to you for emigration and jihad, seeking the reward only from Allah." Allah's Messenger said, "Is one from amongst your parents living?" When the Companion said, "Yes, both are living," the Prophet said, "You mean to say that you seek reward from Allah?" Upon the Companion's saying, "Yes," Allah's Messenger said, "Then go back to your parents and accord them benevolent treatment (for Allah's approval lies herein)."

In another narration a Companion said, "I left my parents who were in tears." The Messenger of Allah said, "Go back to them and make them laugh as you made them weep." Those unfortunate souls who leave their parents elsewhere and abandon them must return to them without delay and must make them laugh as they have made them weep. They must not give way to such empty consolations as nursing homes and must embrace their parents, who perpetually cherished and nestled them, keeping them well away from these places of separation and longing, for their parents wish to be with their children, spring to life with love for their grandchildren, and live in the warmth of a home in which they can share everything.

The Messenger of Allah asked a great many individuals seeking permission for jihad or emigration whether or not their parents were still living, in consideration of their need for care, their loneliness and yearning, old age and weakness. As a result, he sent some of them back to attend to the needs of their parents and gave others various types of counsel. For instance, to Jahima who approached him saying, "O Messenger of Allah! I too want to participate in military expedition and I have come to consult you in this matter," he asked, "Do you have a mother?" Jahima said, "Yes." Allah's Messenger then replied, "Then stay with her, for Paradise is beneath her feet."

READING TEXT
Such Sacrifice

"Can I see my baby?" asked the new mother. A soft bundle was placed in her arms and the happy mother rushed to open the blanket to see the tiny face of her baby. She was left speechless in astonishment at what she saw. The doctor watching the mother and baby hastily turned his face away from them and began looking out the window. The baby had no ears.

Ensuing medical examinations indicated that the baby's hearing had not been affected, but that there was only the absence of ears, which caused disfigurement.

Years passed, the infant grew up and started school. Upon return home from school one day he threw himself in his mother's arms and was sobbing. This was his first great disappointment. Crying, he said, "One of the big kids called me a monstrosity," and continued sobbing.

The small child grew up thus. He was popular among his classmates and was a successful student. He could have even been class captain, if he had only mingled with his peers.

"You must mix with young people," his mother always told him, but at the same time she felt a deep sense of pity and compassion. The young man's father consulted the family doctor about his son's situation.

"Can't something be done," he asked.

The doctor said, "An organ transplant is possible, if a pair of ears can be found."

The search then began for someone who could give up their ears for a young man. Two years later, his father said, "You're going to the hospital, son. Your mother and I have found someone who will give you their ears, but don't forget that this is a secret."

The operation was a great success and now he, too, had ears. His emotional state improving with his new appearance, the youth achieved great success in his academic and social life. He later married and became a diplomat. Many years passed and one day the boy went to his father and asked, "I want to know the person who has done me so much kindness? I haven't been able to do anything for them…"

"I don't think there's anything you can do for them," his father said. "But the agreement is clear. You can't find out right now. Not yet."

This deep secret was kept hidden for years. But one day, the time had come for it to be revealed.

On one of the darkest days of his life, he was waiting with his father beside his mother's body. His father slowly extended his hand to his mother's head and gently pushed back her golden brown hair. His mother had no ears.

Respect for Parents May Help Us to Secure Allah's Forgiveness

The following story as told by our Prophet, peace and blessings be upon him, felicitously stress the importance of showing respect for parents:

> While three persons were walking, rain began to fall and they had to enter a cave in a mountain. A big rock rolled over and blocked the mouth of the cave. They said to each other, 'Invoke Allah with the best deed you have performed (so Allah might remove the rock)'. One of them said, 'O Allah! My parents were old and I used to go out for grazing (my animals). On my return I would milk (the animals) and take the milk in a vessel to my parents to drink. After they had drunk from it, I would give it to my children, family and wife. One day I was delayed and on my return I found my parents sleeping, and I disliked to wake them up. The children were crying at my feet (because of hunger). That state of affairs continued till it was dawn. O Allah! If You regard that I did it for Your sake, then please remove this rock so that we may see the sky.' So, the rock was moved a bit. The second said, 'O Allah! You know that I was in love with a cousin of mine, like the deepest love a man

may have for a woman, and she told me that I would not get my
desire fulfilled unless I paid her one-hundred Dinars (gold pieces).
So, I struggled for it till I gathered the desired amount, and when
I sat in between her legs, she told me to be afraid of Allah, and
asked me not to deflower her except rightfully (by marriage). So, I
got up and left her. O Allah! If You regard that I did it for Your
sake, kindly remove this rock.' So, two-thirds of the rock was
removed. Then the third man said, 'O Allah! No doubt You know
that once I employed a worker for one Faraq (three Sa's) of millet,
and when I wanted to pay him, he refused to take it, so I sowed it
and from its yield I bought cows and a shepherd. After a time that
man came and demanded his money. I said to him: Go to those
cows and the shepherd and take them for they are for you. He asked
me whether I was joking with him. I told him that I was not joking
with him, and all that belonged to him. O Allah! If You regard that
I did it sincerely for Your sake, then please remove the rock.' So,
the rock was removed completely from the mouth of the cave.[7]

The sacrifice the first person mentioned in the *hadith* above made
for his parents was clearly a deed pleasant to Allah. In this context, we
can make the following conclusion: a person who pleases his/her parents will never falter or be overwhelmed with problems. He will be
happy both in this world and in the Hereafter.

As the phrase goes, "As you sow, so shall you reap." People tend to
receive the same treatment from their children as they have given to
their parents. Indeed, the Prophet, peace and blessings be upon him,
drew attention to this fact when he said: "Do favors to your parents so
that your kids may do favors to you... You lead a chaste life so that
your women may lead chaste lives."[8]

Accordingly, those who complain about the treatment they receive
from their children are actually getting their comeuppance for ill-treat-
ing their parents. This is the comeuppance they receive in this world.
The comeuppance in the Hereafter is torment. Indeed, the verse reads:
*"And indeed, the punishment in the Hereafter is more severe and most endur-
ing"* (Ta-Ha 20:127). To avoid this punishment, one should repent as

---

[7] *Sahih al-Bukhari*, Anbiya 50; Buyu, 98; Ijara, 12; Harth, 13, Adab, 5; *Sahih Muslim*,
    Dhikr, 100; *Sunan Abu Dawud*, Buyu, 29.

[8] Al-Tabarani, *Al-Mu'jam al-Awsat*, 1:299; Al-Hakim, *Al-Mustadrak*, 4:171.

soon as possible and treat his/her parents with kindness and set a good example to others in this respect.

READING TEXT
What Are the Duties of a Child toward His or Her Parents?

We see that the Holy Qur'an and our Prophet's *hadith*s attach much importance to kind treatment of parents. This urges us to think what we can do for you them in more concrete terms. We can say that responsibility of children toward their parents can be grouped mainly into two groups: the responsibilities toward our parents as long as they are alive and the responsibilities toward them after they pass away.

1. Our main responsibilities toward our parents when they are still alive:
   a. To visit them;
   b. To address their needs and serve them;
   c. To obey their words as long as they do not tell us to commit a sin or perform a sinful act;
   d. To treat them with love, compassion and tenderness;
   e. To be respectful toward them;
   f. Not to disrupt their sleep or wake them up wantonly;
   g. To ask permission before entering their room;
   h. To work for the guidance of parents to truth;
2. Our main responsibilities toward our parents after they pass away:
   a. To fulfill their wills;
   b. To pray for them and ask Allah to forgive them;
   c. They donate charity on their behalf;
   d. To perform their due worships they couldn't perform, such going to hajj (pilgrimage);
   e. To pay visits to their relatives;
   f. To visit their graves.

Going against or rebelling at parents is considered one of the cardinal sins, and it is certainly an action Allah does not dislike. By severing ties with his/her parents, a person does something that is characteristic of a hypocrite (*munafiq*), not of a Muslim. Indeed, as it describes characteristics of hypocrites in Verses 22 and 23 of the chapter Muhammad, the Holy Qur'an notes that they sever tie with their kinship.

If a person commits the sin of severing ties with parents and relatives, he may be deprived of Allah's mercy and blessing and his prayers may be not be answered, and he may eventually not be entitled to enter Paradise. For this reason, anyone who seeks to attain bliss and happiness both in this world and the next should try to earn the pleasure of his/her parents in the first place. It is interesting note that as they raise us, they do not care for us only one day in a year, such as the "child's day." Instead, they work sacrificially day and night and even until we can stand on own feet. Therefore, our duty is to diligently fulfill the responsibilities our religion imposes on us regarding our parents and work hard to earn their pleasure.[9]

READING TEXT
With All You Are Doing, You Cannot Pay Back the Pain Your Mother Suffered while Giving Birth to You

Muadh ibn Jabal was a Companion of the Prophet, a fortunate person who had attended the spiritual gatherings of the Prophet. Someone asked him, "To what extent is one indebted to his/her parents?" He replied, "You cannot pay back your debts to your parents even if you spend all your wealth?"

* * *

Said ibn Abu Burda narrates a story his father Abu Burda had heard from ibn Umar. One day ibn Umar saw a man from Yemen who was circumambulating the Ka'ba while carrying his mother on his back. "I am a lowly camel for my mother," the man was murmuring. "Do I pay back my debts to my mother by doing so?" he asked ibn Umar. "No, not in the least. With you are doing, you cannot pay back for the pain your mother suffered while giving birth to you," ibn Umar replied.

* * *

---

[9] For detailed information, see Furkan Adil, *Kudsi Varlık Anne-Baba* (Our Dear Parents), İstanbul: Rehber, 2005, pp. 117–159.

A man asked Umar, the second caliph, known for his justice: "I have a mother who no longer can care for herself on her own. I carry her on my back and I help her to take ablution. While doing all these things, I never reproach or taunt her. Do you I pay back my debts to my mother?" "No," replied Umar. "I make myself a saddle beast for her. I am dedicated to her care. How can it be that I still cannot repay my debt toward my mother?" the man asked in amazement. Then, Umar made the following striking observations: "Your mother had already done all those things for you. But as she was doing them, she was doing them so that you live and grow up. But as you care for your mother, you are waiting for her death."

* * *

Umar saw a man who was carrying his mother as they circumambulated the Ka'ba. While carrying her mother, he was saying: "I am carrying my mother on my back. But it was actually her who was the porter. She suckled me and fed me abundantly." Seeing this event, Umar remarked: "Seeing this man's self-sacrifice, I realized better that my mother had extensive rights over me. Acting like this man would seem nicer to me than having red camels (the most precious breed of camels)."

By saying so, Umar expressed his longing. He indicated that he would be eager to carry his mother on his back if she were alive. To make an analogy, he said he would prefer to carry his mother on his back rather than to have luxury cars.

* * *

Abu Nawfal narrates:

One day a man visited Umar and said he had committed a murder.

"Alas. It's a pity. Did you commit the murder intentionally or by accident?" Umar asked. When the man said that it was an accident, Umar asked if his parents were alive. The man replied that his father was alive. And Umar gave him the following advice: "Go at once to your father and serve him. Do everything you can do to earn his pleasure."

Later, Umar commented: "By Allah, if his mother were alive and if he served her, this would give me hope that the fire of Hell will never devour him."

* * *

Abdullah ibn Abbas once said, "I don't know anything more effective method for getting closer to Allah than being kind to the mother and earning her pleasure."

* * *

Kindness to parents is like a mount taking us to Paradise. A believer should try to win the hearts of his/her parents in order to be entitled to Paradise or attain Paradise easily. If they are not pleased with us, there is the risk of not being among the first to enter Paradise. As a matter of fact, earning the pleasure of parents amounts to earning the pleasure of Allah. To break their hearts is to offend Allah the Almighty. People who hurt the feelings of their parents will be denied the bliss of being among the first to enter Paradise. Aisha, the mother of believers, the mother of believers, may Allah be pleased with her, narrates: In his dream, the Most Noble Prophet entered Paradise and heard someone reciting the Holy Qur'an. "Who is this?" he asked those in Paradise. "It is Haritha ibn an-Numan," they replied.

He was one of the veteran Helpers (the Ansar) who had attended all battles including Badr, Uhud, and the Trench. He was a distinguished Companion, known for his virtues. Our Prophet had provided the following explanation for his admission to Paradise, although he had so many other virtues:

"That is because of his kindness to parents."[10]

After repeating this sentence for three times, he added: "Haritha was most kind to his mother."

This is a thought-provoking lesson from our Prophet about where to find a key to Paradise. To regain our lost Paradise, we must extend our hands to our parents with kindness and we should not stay close them so that they can take us to Paradise.

---

[10] Abu Ya'la, *Al-Musnad*, 7/399; *Sunan an-Nasa'i*, 5:65.

QUESTIONS

1. In which chapter in the Holy Qur'an does Allah enjoin us not to say "Ugh!" to our parents?
   a. Al-Isra, Verses 23–24
   b. Al-Baqarah, Verses 285–286
   c. Yasin, Verses 44–45
   d. Al Imran, Verses 66–67

2. Which of the following verses tells believers to treat their parents with kindness, saying, "And say: 'My Lord, have mercy on them even as they cared for me in childhood'"?
   a. Fatiha, Verse 2   b. Al-Kawthar, Verse 1
   c. Al-Fil, Verse 3   d. Al-Isra, Verse 24

3. Which of the Names of Allah is best manifested in parents?
   a. Al-Jalil (The All-Majestic)
   b. Al-Mutakabbir (The One Who has exclusive right for all greatness)
   c. Ar-Rahman (The All-Merciful) and Ar-Rahim (The All-Compassionate)
   d. Al-Jamil (The All-Gracious)

4. Who is the Companion our Prophet saw in Paradise reciting the Holy Qur'an as a reward for his kindness to parents?
   a. Haritha ibn al-Numan   b. Ali ibn Abi Talib
   c. Abu Hurayra   d. Zayd ibn Haritha

5. Who is the Companion who said, "I don't know anything more effective method for getting closer to Allah than being kind to the mother and earning her pleasure"?
   a. Abdullah ibn Umar   b. Abdullah ibn Amr
   c. Abdullah ibn Mas'ud   d. Abdullah ibn Abbas

3.

FRIENDSHIP AND FELLOWSHIP

"A man is upon the religion of his best friend, so let one of you look at whom he befriends." (*Sunan Abu Dawud,* 4833).

People are social creatures. They need other people in order to survive. This is a Divine law. This is the way Allah created man. Therefore, every human being needs other people in order to overcome material or immaterial obstacles in life.

There are some people to whom we feel ourselves closer. They are our friends. They come to help us in times of need. They act like guides for us.

Importance Our Religion Attaches to Friendship and Fellowship

In religious literature, the word "bosom friend" or "confidant" is closely associated with the concepts of loyalty, fidelity, brotherhood, and spiritual gathering. A person who shows us loyalty and friendship is a "friend." Friendship is a profound bond between people based on affinity, attachment, and intimacy.

A life without friends is inconceivable. Life becomes meaningful thanks to friendships. Friends are particularly important for people who subscribe to a noble cause.

Friends in the Holy Qur'an

The Holy Qur'an makes frequent references to friendship by using the word "wali" (guardian, confidant, or helper). Decreeing in the Qur'an that "the believers, both men and women: they are guardians, confidants, and helpers of one another," Allah asserts that friendship is/should be a characteristic of believers.[11]

Indeed, believers are essentially sisters and brothers.[12] In this context, the friendship between the Helpers (Ansar) and the Emigrants (Muhajirun) during the time of the Prophet was legendary. Referring to this epic friendship, the Holy Qur'an notes that Allah reconciled the hearts of the people who were enemies and thanks to Allah's favor, they became like brothers.[13]

The Qur'an also uses the word "khullah" (close friendship) in referring to fellowship. *Khullah* means profound friendship that has penetrated deep in one's heart and become established. Using this word, Allah says He accepted Abraham as a close and trusted friend (*khalil*).[14]

For believers, an ideal friend is the one with whom our Lord and our Prophet would be content. Allah refers to such people as "excellent they are for companions" in the Holy Qur'an:

> Whoever obeys Allah and the Messenger (as they must be obeyed), then those are (and in the Hereafter will be, in Paradise) in the company of those whom Allah has favored (with the perfect guidance)—the Prophets, and the truthful ones (loyal to Allah's cause and truthful in whatever they do and say), and the witnesses (those who see the hidden Divine truths and testify thereto with their lives), and the righteous ones (in all their deeds and sayings, and dedicated to setting everything right). How excellent they are for companions! (An-Nisa 4:69).

For this reason, we need to make sure that our friends are honest and straightforward people. Indeed, this is what Allah enjoins us to do: *"O you who believe! Keep from disobedience to Allah in reverence for Him and piety, and keep the company of the truthful (those who are also faithful to their covenant with Allah)"* (at-Tawbah 9:119). Our friends should be benevolent and dutiful people. In the following prayer, our Lord teaches us that as we choose our friends, we must make sure that they are righ-

---

[11] At-Tawbah 9:71.

[12] Al-Hujurat 49:10.

[13] Al Imran 3:103.

[14] An-Nisa 4:125.

teous people: *"My Lord! Grant me true, wise judgment, and join me with the righteous"* (ash-Shu'ara 26:83).

True, our friends must be auspicious. Satan calls on people to make friends with him and devilish people. This is expressed in the following verse: *"And (likewise) those who spend their wealth (in charity or other good cause) to make a show of it to people (so as to be praised by them) when they believe neither in Allah nor in the Last Day: Whoever has Satan for a comrade, how evil a comrade he is!"* (an-Nisa, 4:38). Another verse describes how the people who are comrades of Satan deceive other people with various tricks to lead them astray.[15]

Beloved Friend

I don't know if I have made any progress, my dear friend!
Or if I have been strayed in a foreign land, my dear friend!

I am exhausted, bedraggled, slovenly, and enfeebled;
Should my doldrums linger on like Jacob, my dear friend!

My roads are blocked by mountains and deserts,
Should the pale roses in my hands fade away, my dear friend?

The road is getting steep and my flaws are becoming manifest,
My days are getting darker; should it stay in this state, my dear friend?

Slightest grace and protection is all I need,
If you don't help me, should I cry one, my dear friend?

You order us to keep a good opinion and expect forgiveness;
But if you don't forgive me, should I burn on?[16]

Friendship and Fellowship in the Prophetic Traditions

An examination of the Prophetic Traditions reveals that the Messenger of Allah attached great importance to friendship and fellowship. A believer's friendship with their fellow believer must be oriented toward Divine pleasure and approval. That is to say, the believer loves their fellow believer for the sake of Allah and establishes their friendship and

---

15 Fussilat 41:25.
16 Gülen, M. Fethullah, *Kırık Mızrap*, Istanbul: Nil, 2006, p. 282.

fellowship with them on this basis. In one of his hadith, Allah's Messenger articulates this truth as follows: "The strongest bond of belief is friendship for the sake of Allah and opposition for His sake, love for the sake of Allah and disfavor for His sake."

Whilst sincere friendships established for the sake of Allah continue for all eternity, those based on self-interest can end even while in the world. Love and friendship for Allah's sake can never be dependent on self-interest. The Qur'anic verse, *"Those who are intimate friends (in the world) will be enemies one to another on that Day, except the God-revering, pious"* (az-Zukhruf 43:67), vividly expresses the fact that friendships other than those formed for the sake of Allah can turn into enmity in the Hereafter.

Moreover, a hadith describing one of those people to be given protection on the Day of Reckoning wherein there is no shade save the shade of Allah as, "those who love one another for the sake of Allah," reveals the reward of those people who love each other for His sake. Indeed, the believer must form friendships for the sake of Allah and their friend must take them to Him. A friend who takes one to Allah is most certainly an auspicious friend. Allah's Messenger relates the good friend in one Prophetic Tradition by means of the following excellent similitude: "The similitude of good company and that of bad company is that of the owner of musk and of the one blowing the bellows. The owner of musk would either offer you some free of charge, or you would buy it from him, or you smell its pleasant fragrance; and as for the one who blows the bellows (i.e., the blacksmith), he either burns your clothes or you get from it a repugnant smell."

Saying, "A person is upon the religion of their friend," Allah's Messenger demands from us to be careful in our choice of friends, as the good friend takes one to Paradise, while a bad one takes one to the pits of the Fire.

Fellowship resembles a single spirit in two bodies. Our friends are our capital in both this world and the Hereafter. They are treasures enabling us to attain happiness in both this world and in the Hereafter. The Messenger of Allah expresses this reality in the following hadith:

Umar ibn al-Khattab, may Allah be pleased with him, reported the Prophet as saying: "There are people from the servants of Allah who are neither Prophets nor martyrs; the Prophets and martyrs will envy them on the Day of Resurrection for their rank from Allah, the Most High."

They (the people) asked: 'Tell us, O Messenger of Allah, who are they?' He replied: 'They are people who love one another for the spirit of Allah (i.e. the Qur'an), without having any mutual kinship and giving property to one. I swear by Allah, their faces will glow and they will be (sitting) in (pulpits of) light. They will have no fear (on the Day) when the people will have fear, and they will not grieve when the people will grieve.'

He then recited the following Qur'anic verse: *'Know well that the friends (saintly servants) of Allah—they will have no fear (both in this world and the next, for they will always find My help and support with them), nor will they grieve.'*[17]

READING TEXT
Two Close Friends

Akif and Ali were very close friends with great affection for each other. Those around them envied the relationship of the devoted companions. The friends believed that doing charitable deeds was an effective way of amending errors. When a person is called to do good deeds by a person of goodwill, it reminds him of truth, and prevents him from straying from the path of righteousness.

One day, Akif wrote a moral contract. He called it "the agreement of goodwill" and it was meant to invoke kindness, inform friends of faults and help to rectify mistakes.

"I want us both to sign an agreement," Akif said.

"What kind of an agreement?" Ali asked.

"I am permitting you to inform me of my mistakes, or anything I do personally that you think is wrong."

"Okay, but I can only accept this on one condition.

You must inform me of my mistakes, too."

---

[17] *Sunan Abu Dawud*, Book 24, Hadith 112.

"Okay, I agree."

The friends signed the contract, and became a "spirit of goodwill" to each other.

Many years passed, and their relationship was still as strong as ever. Then, because of work, Akif had to move to a different city, which grieved them both. The companions comforted one another, and promised to visit frequently. Theirs was a friendship for life.

After a month had passed, Ali missed his friend very much. Whenever Ali mentioned his name in conversation, his eyes would fill with tears. He could not wait any longer to see his dear friend, so he decided to visit.

On the way, he noticed a strange man. The man was sitting on the roadside, and looked as if he was trying to say something to him. Ali walked over to the man and greeted him. The man asked:

"Where are you off to, young man?"

"I am going to visit my friend," Ali replied.

"Your friend must have done you a great favor, and now you are going to thank him."

"No, I have nothing to thank him for. I love him for the sake of Allah and I am visiting him for the sake of Allah."

"How nice. I am going to tell you a secret. Now listen to me carefully. I am an angel sent to you by Allah. Know that just as you love your friend for the sake of Allah, Allah also loves you dearly."

Who Are Friends of Allah?

The Holy Qur'an tells us that Allah the Almighty is the guardian, confidant, and friend of believers.[18] Does this friendship encompass all believers? Are only some believers who have certain qualifications friends of Allah? Allah befriends those who properly believe in Him and perform deeds that please Allah.[19]

In other words, Allah is a guardian and confidant of God-revering servants who are aware of, and act responsibly in regard of, their servi-

---

[18] Al-Baqarah 2:257; Al Imran 3:68.
[19] Al-An'am 6:127.

tude to Allah and who properly revere Allah.[20] Allah is the true confidant. Man does not have any true guardian/confidant or helper other than Allah.[21]

Above, we have noted that our Lord will befriend those who perform righteous deeds. What are these righteous deeds? The Holy Qur'an answers this question as follows: being a Muslim, believing in Allah and the Prophet in the way Islam describes, performing our Prescribed Prayers, paying prescribed alms, and having the spiritual excellence to account for our actions.[22]

At this point, let us ask a question: are there people who lose the friendship of Allah or who lose the friendship of Allah for their wrong choices or evil deeds?

Allah is not a guardian or confidant of those who are misguided or who go astray. There are some people who persistently stick to the obvious error even if Allah's Prophets call on them to return to the straight path. Allah leaves such people to their misguided preferences and they cannot find any other guardian or confidant.[23]

Allah is not also a friend or helper of those who arrogantly refuse to be His servant[24] as well as of those people who perform evil deeds.[25]

Allah the Almighty is not a friend (guardian) of those who fall into unbelief after having entered the fold of Islam and of hypocrites who pretend to be believers although they are not believers. They will not find for themselves any guardian or helper on Earth.[26]

Allah is not a guardian or helper of those who disbelieve Him or who turn their backs on the true religion or those wrongdoers who acts unjustly on Earth.[27]

---

[20] Al-Jathiyah 45:19; al-A'raf 7:196.
[21] At-Tawbah 9:116; al-An'am 6:70; al-Kahf 18:26; al-Ankabut 29:22.
[22] Al-Maedah 5:55–56; al-Baqarah 2:112.
[23] Ash-Shura 42:44; al-Isra 17:97.
[24] An-Nisa 4:173; al-Jathiyah 45:7–10.
[25] An-Nisa 4:123.
[26] At-Tawbah 9:74; al-Ahzab 33:17.
[27] Ash-Shura 42:8; Hud 11 20.

Why Should I Have Good Friends?

"I observe that whenever I spend time with people who do not perform their Prescribed Prayers, my faculties tend to be blunted," says
Islamic scholar Imam Sharani. For this reason, a believer should take
into consideration what he may lose by befriending irreligious people,
unscrupulous people, or those whose hearts are blackened. If he can make
this assessment, he will realize that he may keep company with the irreligious people only with the purpose of guiding them to the Straight
Path. While we may choose to keep our company with such people,
we should avoid their friendship just for entertainment value.

The radioactive spill from the evil people who do not pay respect to
what is religiously forbidden may adversely affect the hearts and minds
of believers. The Holy Qur'an indicates that when the people who go
to Hell are asked about what brought them to Hell, they will reply: *"We
were not of those who prayed (who turn to Allah in sincere worship). Nor did
we use to feed the destitute. We used to plunge (in falsehood and sin) together with those who plunged (in it). And we used to deny the (coming of the)
Day of Judgment"* (al-Muddathir 74:40–46).

They take wrong people for friends in this world and their friends
lead them astray. Sadi Shirazi describes this situation as follows: "A bad
friend is worse than a black snake. If you come under his influence, he
will drag you into Hell. A good friend, on the other hand, takes you
to Paradise." So we must move away from bad friends as we would run
away from a black snake. Indeed, the Holy Qur'an tells us that those
who take bad people for friends in this world will cry out regretfully in
the Hereafter as follows: *"On that Day, the wrongdoer will bite at his
hands, saying (with remorse), 'Oh, would that I had taken a way in the company of the Messenger. Oh, woe is me! Would that I had not taken so-and-
so for a friend!'"* (al-Furqan 25:27–28).

Believers should have good friends and keep company with righteous
person people. Having good friends is very important as no one can
stand on his/her feet alone at all times. A person cannot act both as the
central pole and the stakes of a tent. When he acts as the central pole,
his friends should act as the stakes so that his tent of existence can be
properly erected. Only in this way can he stand. Stones of a dome do

not fall down when they lean against each other. If they stop leaning on each other, even the smallest of them will fall down. In this context, our noble Prophet said: "A lonely person is Satan. Two people are Satan. (Two people can still agree on evil things). But three people are a community."[28]

If our Prophet advises us to live in such an atmosphere, then we must seek to create such an atmosphere. This means we must make the atmosphere become like us. Then, our duty is to stick to righteous friends at all times. In this way, when we come close to committing a mistake, they will caution and correct us. Most of the time, we would be embarrassed by them so that we can suppress our evil emotions.

When a righteous believer cautions his brother in religion, saying, "You are not being careful about what to look or see," he will first be shocked, but this is not important. Thanks to that warning, he will restore himself to good action. This is the reward of keeping company with good friends.

READING TEXT
Today, My Best Friend Slapped Me across My Face

Two friends were traveling in the desert. At some point, there was a dispute between them, and one of the friends slapped the other across his face. The man who was slapped on the face was hurt and his heart was broken, but he said nothing. Only he wrote the following sentence on the sand:

"Today, my best friend slapped me across my face."

They kept on walking. The water they were carrying with them was diminishing. Luckily, they made it to an oasis. They drank water to their heart's content and they filled their flasks. Then, they decided to swim in the water. While swimming, the man who was slapped across the face got trapped in some slime. He was going under at every second. But his friend rushed to save him. After being saved by his best friend, he went to a rock and wrote the following sentence on the rock:

---

[28] *Sunan Abu Dawud*, Jihad, 79; *Sunan at-Tirmidhi*, Jihad, 4.

"Today my best friend saved my life."

The other man asked:

"When I hurt you, you wrote it on the sand. Now, you wrote it on the rock. Why?"

His friend replied: "When someone hurts us, we need to write it on the sand so that the winds of forgiveness can easily remove it. But when someone does us a favor, we must engrave it on the rock so that the winds of rage or revenge cannot remove it."[29]

The Friendship in the World Will Resume in the Hereafter

In interpreting and explaining the verse, *"Those who are intimate friends (in the world) will be enemies one to another on that Day, except the God-revering, pious,"* (az-Zukhruf, 43:47), famous interpreter Qurtubi narrates relatives the following incident from Ath-Tha'labi:

"There were two friends who were unbelievers and two friends who were believers. One of the believers died and he was told he was entitled to enter Paradise. Remembering the man who was his bosom friend in the world, he said: 'O Allah, the so-and-so is my friend. He would tell me to obey You and Your Prophet and he would forbid evil deeds and he would give the glad tiding that I would return to You. O Allah, do not let him go astray after I left him and give him the blessings and favors you gave unto me. Let him earn Your pleasure just as I earned Your pleasure.'

"Then, the other believer died and their souls came together and they were told: 'Let each of you tell what he wishes to tell about the other.' Both indicated that they were pleased with each other, and Allah said, 'What good brothers you are! What good friends you are! What good confidants you are!'

"This time, one of the two unbelievers died and when he was told that he would go to Hell, he remembered his bosom friend in the world and said: 'O Allah, my friend so-and-so would enjoin me to revolt

---

[29] Çiftkaya, Murat, *Gökkuşağı Öyküleri* (Rainbow Stories), İstanbul: Timaş, 2003, p. 27.

against You and Your Prophet and forbid good deeds and he would say that I would not return to You. O Allah, do not guide him to the Straight Path so that You give him the punishment You gave to me.'

"Referring to them, Allah said: "What evil brothers you are! What evil friends you are! What evil confidants you are!' Then, they started to curse each other."[30]

It follows that the friendship and companionship in this world resume in the Hereafter. So we must never forget that our friendships here will continue in the Hereafter. Accordingly, we can call our friendships as "otherworldly friendships."

Anas ibn Malik, a Companion of the Prophet, narrates:

"When the people of Paradise enter Paradise and settle in their allocated places (mansions), they miss their sisters and brothers in religion and want to see them. As they think about seeing them, their seats immediately travel to the mansions of their friends.

"When they come together, they start to talk about their memories back in the world. One of them says: 'O brother, do you remember the time when we had prayed to Allah sincerely in the such-and-such spiritual gathering or in the such-and-such mosque (we had recited the Holy Qur'an; we have listened to the sermon)? Allah had absolved us there.'"[31]

For this reason, we must be very careful in choosing our friends. We must not forget that our choice will apply not only to this world, but also to the next. Those who fail to befriend good people may ruin their life both in this world and the next.

READING TEXT
Important Criteria on Friendship and Companionship

1. Man's need for faithful companions is not more frivolous or negligible than his essential needs. Being among a secure and peaceful circle of friends means finding safety against many hazards and dangers.

---

[30] Qurtubi, *Al-Jami li-Ahkam al-Qur'an*, 16:109.
[31] Suyuti, *Al-Fath al-Kabir*, 1:79.

2. Wise people, upon seeing that a friendship has become damaged, immediately remove the cause of discontent and restore good relations. Even wiser are those who strive to avoid or prevent disagreement with their friends in the first place.

3. Love and good relations between friends continue as long as they understand each other, practice self-denial, and make sacrifices within permissible limits. Friendship between those who cannot renounce their interests and preferences for the sake of their friends cannot endure.

4. We are loyal and faithful to our friends to the extent we share their troubles as well as their joys. If we cannot weep when our friends weep and rejoice when they rejoice, we cannot be regarded as faithful friends.

5. Those who maintain a friendship with one who has fallen on hard times are true, loyal friends. Those who do not support their friends during their misfortune have nothing to do with friendship.

6. Those who tend to disagree and quarrel with their friends have few friends. Anyone who wants many and faithful friends should refrain from unnecessary controversies with them.

7. Friendship pertains to one's heart and its sincerity. Those who think they can gain another's friendship through deception and hypocrisy only deceive themselves. Even if some simple-minded people are taken in by their hypocrisy and flattery, they will not be able to sustain a long-lasting friendship.[32]

---

[32] Gülen, M. Fethullah, *Pearls of Wisdom*, New Jersey: The Light, 2005, pp. 80–81.

QUESTIONS

1. Which of the phrases below best fits the blanks in the sentence, "The friendship between the .... and .... during the time of the Prophet was legendary"?
   a. The Ansar (Helpers) – The Emigrants (Muhajirun)
   b. Mecca – Medina
   c. Ali – Umar
   d. Uthman – Ali

2. According to the Holy Qur'an, "whoever obeys Allah and the Messenger" are in the company of which group below?
   a. The Prophets whom Allah has favored
   b. The truthful ones
   c. The witnesses
   d. All of the above

3. Who is described by the Holy Qur'an as the worst of comrades?
   a. Satan   b. The jinn
   c. Fairies   d. None

4. What should a person rely on in choosing his/her friends?
   a. Carnal desires   b. Family preferences
   c. Allah's pleasure   d. Worldly benefits

5. Which Islamic school said that a person's spiritual faculties will be blunted if he keeps company with the people who do not perform ritual Prayers?
   a. Imam al-Ghazali   b. Imam Sharani
   c. Imam Malik   d. Imam Shafi

6. Which of the following is not related to the concept of fellowship?
   a. Friend   b. Love
   c. Beloved   d. Partner

7. Which of the following concepts is not associated with the concept of friendship?

a. Close friendship (*khullah* or *khillah*)

b. Brotherhood (*ukhuwah*)

c. Guardian or confidant (*wali*)

d. Enmity

8. Which chapter of the Holy Qur'an has a verse indicating that all friendships except those that seek to earn Allah's pleasure will turn into enmities in the Hereafter?

a. Al-Fatiha   b. Az-Zukhruf

c. Al-Ikhlas   d. Al-Asr

9. To whom does the *hadith* liken good and bad friends?

a. The seller of musk and the one who blows the blacksmith's bellows

b. The seller of musk and the imam

c. The one who blows the blacksmith's bellows and the farmer

d. The seller of musk and the farmer

10. Which of the following sentences is wrong?

a. Allah is not a friend of arrogant people.

b. Allah is not a friend of evildoers.

c. Allah is not a friend of hypocrites.

d. Allah is not a friend of the oppressed.

4.

BENEVOLENCE

"The upper (giving) hand is better than the lower (taking) hand."[33]

Benevolence Is Part of Believers' Ethics

Benevolence is essentially a fundamental principle for believers. Indeed, benevolence becomes part of believers' dispositions. For believers, it is virtuous to give in charity and help other people to the extent their financial capabilities allow. In the Holy Qur'an, our Lord promises Paradise as a reward for those who act in this way: *"Allah has bought from the believers their selves and wealth because Paradise is for the*m" (at-Tawbah 9:111).

Anything we spend, even if we spend it to earn Allah's pleasure, eventually becomes beneficial to us in the form of Divine rewards. Indeed, Allah will provide us with complete comeuppance for our actions. This is confirmed in another verse in the Qur'an:

> (O people,) whatever good you spend (in charity and other good causes) is to your own benefit, and (as believers) you do not spend but in search of Allah's 'Face' (seeking to be worthy of His approval). Whatever good you spend will be repaid to you in full, and you will not be wronged. (Al-Baqarah 2:272).

In another verse, believers are called on not only to spend in charity, but also to spend from the best of what they have: *"You will never*

---

[33] *Sahih Muslim*, Zakah, 97, (1036); *Sunan at-Tirmidhi*, Zuhd, 32, (2344).

be able to attain godliness and virtue until you spend of what you love (in Allah's cause, or to provide sustenance for the needy)" (Al Imran 3:192).

Benevolence is one of the pillars of our religion. Benevolence may take the form of prescribed purifying alms (*zakah*), charity of fast-breaking (*sadaqatu'l-fitr*), spending in the way of Allah (*infaq*), giving loans to other people, eliminating material or immaterial troubles of a brother or sister in religion, helping the elderly, sharing one's allowance with one's friends, etc. Our Lord makes it clear that He will help us on condition that we help His servants. Our Prophet underlines this fact as follows: "Whoever removes a worldly grief from a believer, Allah will remove from him one of the grievances of the Day of Resurrection. And whoever alleviates the need of a needy person, Allah will alleviate his needs in this world and the Hereafter. And Allah will aid His slave so long as he aids his brother."[34]

We Should Make Benevolence Our Habit

In this world where material values dominate the social scene, we need to bring forth the spiritual values so that a balance should be restored between material and immaterial values. When this balance is disrupted, it is impossible to attain social peace. Indeed, the world is full of nations that have abandoned spiritual values in pursuit of material achievements; they have attained what they were looking for, but they have ended up being crushed under the weight of those material achievements. In these countries, people tend to lead completely individual lives without spiritual values such as caring or helping others or extending a helping hand to the destitute.

On the other hand, believers are equipped with the Allah's morality and therefore, are always helpful. They readily use their resources to ensure that others may live in peace. In other words, benevolence has become a natural part of a believer's disposition in all respects.

One way to make benevolence part of human nature is to familiarize our children with it at an early age. Believers should train their children with a benevolence-oriented program that can instill in them such

---

34   *Sahih al-Bukhari*, Mazalim, 3.

an altruism that they can give their coats or shoes to their friends who are in need of them even if they are shivering in the freezing cold. In this way, a sense of sacrificial helpfulness should be etched into their hearts.

This can be achieved by teaching our children how to give in charity. In this context, if we plan to give gifts to some people, we may do it while our children witness it or we may give them through our children. By showing practical examples of charity, we may help our children to develop a preliminary sense of benevolence. In this way, we can raise people who are aware of and concerned about the problems of Muslims all around the world, and we will witness that our efforts are not wasted.

Taking into consideration the fact that there will always be factors that would prevent people from aiding others, believers should not wait for the time when they will have ample opportunities to help others. Rather, they should make it their habit to help others within their capabilities. We should not forget that we will be accountable to Allah only with regard to what we fail to do within our current capabilities, not with respect to what we may or may not do in future.

Our Lord enjoins us to *"help one another in virtue and goodness, and righteousness and piety, and (not to) help one another in sinful, iniquitous acts and hostility"* (al-Maedah 5:2). Given the fact that Islam keeps the scope of good deeds extremely wide open to include a range of deeds ranging from paying the prescribed purifying alms to smiling at one's sister or brother in religion, it is clear that the definition of benevolence is kept considerably comprehensive in our religion.

Everyone Should Is Responsible for Aiding Others according to Their Capacity

Just as they have certain bodily duties, virtually everyone has responsibilities regarding what they possess. These responsibilities apply to our current situation, not to some imagined situation in future. So we cannot postpone our responsibilities regarding what we possess for the time being. In other words, everyone is supposed to perform their responsibilities with what they have at the moment or with what Allah the

Almighty has endowed them. Therefore, believers should try to earn Allah's pleasure by helping the poor according to their financial capacities, and they should seek ways to please Allah using what they have.

In our time, everyone should find ways to make contributions, according to their capacities, to the efforts to spread the word about our Lord and our Prophet everywhere around the world. Some of us may make small contributions while others may donate their wealth to this project so that the overall effect will be beneficial to all of us. A person who donates a small amount to be used in such efforts will get as much reward as those who donate much more money.

Indeed, Allah appreciates quality, not quantity. In this context, Bediüzzaman Said Nursi says, "A minute sincere act is preferable to masses of insincere ones." For this reason, sometimes a small amount of donation may outweigh the entire wealth donated. Accordingly, in addition to being eager to spend our money in the path of Allah, we must be careful about being sincere while giving our money.

Moreover, we need to take care that we spend of what we love. Indeed, the verse reading, *"You will never be able to attain godliness and virtue until you spend of what you love (in Allah's cause, or to provide sustenance for the needy),"* (Al Imran 3:92) refers to this truth. In this context, Anas ibn Malik, a Companion of the Prophet, tells the following story:

"Abu Talha was one of the wealthy notables of the Ansar. His favorite property was Bayruha, which was opposite the Prophet's Mosque (Masjid an-Nabawi). The Messenger of Allah used to enter it and drink its sweet water.

"When the verse, *'You will never be able to attain godliness and virtue until you spend of what you love,'* was sent down, Abu Talha went to the Messenger of Allah and said, 'O Messenger of Allah, Allah the Almighty says, *"You will never be able to attain godliness and virtue until you spend of what you love."* The property I love the most is Bayruha. It is sadaqa (charity) for Allah whose goodness I hope for and I hope that it will be stored up for me with Allah the Almighty. O Messenger of Allah, dispose of it in whatever way Allah shows you is the best.'

"The Messenger of Allah said: 'Excellent! That is a profitable property. I have heard what you have said and I think that you should give it to your relatives.' So Abu Talha divided it among his relatives and cousins."[35]

It is clear from this *hadith* that by spending of what they love in the path of Allah, believers invite Divine bliss and favors and set off on a path leading to Allah's pleasure. This behavior pleases both other people and Allah.

The Generosity of Abu Aqil

Among the Companions, there was a courageous man called Abu Aqil, one of the most honored residents of Medina. Despite his own poverty, Abu Aqil gave his possessions to the Prophet to distribute to the poor, and was ill-treated and reviled by the Hypocrites. Ignoring them, he continued to roam the bazaars of Medina with a rope around his neck, earning a living by carrying loads from one place to another. He would earn four or five coins a day, and gave half to the poor, and half to the Prophet. In an attempt to create animosity between Abu Aqil and the people, the hypocrites said, "Allah is in no need of his charity!" to make him the target of criticism.

Indicating their evil actions, and complimenting Abu Aqil on his behavior, the Qur'an says:

> They taunt the believers, who give for Allah's sake more than they are duty-bound to give, as well as those who can find nothing to give except their hard toil, and they scoff at them. Allah causes their scoffing to rebound on themselves, and for them is a painful punishment. (At-Tawbah 9:79).

When Abu Aqil carried loads around the bazaars, he gave generously and fulfilled his duty. Indeed, he will reap the rewards for his actions in the Hereafter.

What Is the Benefit of Helpfulness to Ourselves?

Munificence does not give rise to financial loss as it may seem; rather, it has many benefits including spiritual as well as material gains. Gen-

---

[35] *Sahih Muslim*, Zakah, 42, 43.

erosity not only earns one prestige in social life, but also affords him/ her protection for his/her life and property. Generosity is a way to seek for Divine mercy and it also paves the way to abundance and bounty. Therefore, generosity brings not only spiritual, but also material satisfaction. Some of the benefits benevolence can be listed as follows:

1. Benevolence Boosts Prestige

Generous and altruistic people earn respectability within the community. As these virtues help believers to get closer to Allah, Allah makes these believers become favorite among His servants. Here is a true story:

During the time when Umar was the Caliph, believers were winning victories and earning huge amounts of spoils in wars. Umar used to favor certain Companions such as Abu Ubayda, Muadh ibn Jabal and Hudhayfa ibn al-Yaman. People couldn't understand Umar's specific sympathy toward these Companions. "Why does Umar address Abu Ubayda as 'my brother'? Why does he like to talk to these people who have nothing but a slim mattress? Why is Muadh ibn Jabal, a young man, treated as among the notables of the Ansar and Muhajirun? Why is Hudhayfa treated as an eminent and distinguished person?" they would ask. Umar decided to teach these people a lesson.

He sent each a pouch of golden coins with envoys. The envoys witnessed that the Companions immediately gave all of those coins to the poor. All of these three Companions did the same thing, showing to the people how Umar was right in holding them in high esteem.[36]

Yet they were living in poverty and deprivation. For instance, Abu Ubayda had participated in an expedition against Heraclius in Syria, and he could earn money only to pay for his needs for two days.

Indeed, Umar went near Damascus and asked the commanders of the Islamic army, "Where is my brother Abu Ubayda?" "He is about to come," they replied. Soon, Abu Ubayda came, riding a camel with ropes, and he greeted the people there, and went directly his home without lingering there much. He was carrying only a sword, a shield, and rations. Seeing his miserable state, Umar could not hold back his

---

[36]   Al-Asqalani, *Al-Isaba*, 1: 469.

tears. Then, he went to him, and asked: "Why don't you look after your-self? Why don't earn some money?" His answer would surprise Umar even more: "O leader of believers, everything is clear. What I have suf-fices me."[37]

Witnessing Abu Ubayda's contentedness (*istighna*), Umar delivered the following judgment, "This world has changed all of us except you."[38] Of course, they wouldn't be changed by the life in this world as they hated taking something from other people. This was the outcome of the sense of equilibrium Islam had instilled in their hearts. So believers should refrain from taking, but rush to give.

Indeed, benevolence is conducive to love and familiarity between the helper and the helped. When we help people by providing them with financial support, we also help them to get rid of the negative sen-timents such as hatred, jealousy, and antagonism against the rich peo-ple. They will learn that the rich people are giving the poor their due and helping other people in line with Islam's injunctions.

2. Benevolence Invites Blessings and Abundance in Wealth

Several verses and *hadith*s make it clear that by spending in the path of Allah, our wealth will not diminish, but increase thanks to Divine blessings. For instance, Abu Bakr spent all of his wealth in the path of Allah for many times, but Allah helped him to earn his wealth once again in each case. Indeed, when spend part of our wealth to help the poor, this will trigger Divine bounty, making our wealth increase just as a pruned tree becomes more vivid and productive. This truth is explained in the Holy Qur'an as follows:

The parable of those who spend their wealth in Allah's cause is like that of a grain that sprouts seven ears, and in every ear, there are a hun-dred grains. Allah multiplies for whom He wills. Allah is All-Embrac-ing (with His mercy), All-Knowing. (Al-Baqarah 2:261).

---

[37] Al-Asqalani, *Al-Isaba*, 3:589.

[38] Ibn al-Athir, *Usd al-Ghabah*, 5:206.

Our great ones likened the property that was not spent as charity to the water that becomes stinging after standing still for a long time. Sadi Shirazi puts it elegantly:

"Don't think you'll rise by collecting money. The standing water stinks. Try to donate it in charity. The sky helps the flowing water. It sends rain and floods and won't let it run dry."

Rumi illustrates the same point as follows:

"When you sow crops, you first empty the warehouse, but you eventually fill it with more crops. If you keep your crops in the warehouse instead of sowing, you make them food for mice."

In a *hadith*, the Messenger of Allah, peace and blessings be upon him, touches on some principles which we may call as the worldview of believers, noting that spending wealth in charity or alms will not lead to a decrease in wealth:

"The three things which I swear to be true are that a man's property does not become less on account of sadaqa; that when a man is wronged and bears it patiently Allah will give him greater honor on that account; and that when a man opens a door towards begging Allah opens for him a door towards poverty. The thing I am going to tell you which you must keep in mind is this. The world has only four types of people:

"1. A man whom Allah provides with property and knowledge, in which he fears his Lord and joins ties of relationship, acting in it toward Allah as is due to Him, this man being in the most excellent station.

"2. A man whom Allah provides with knowledge but not with property, who says with a sincere intention that if he had property he would act as so and so does, their reward being equal.

"3. A man whom Allah provides with property but not with knowledge, in which he acts in a random manner ignorantly, not fearing his Lord respecting it, or using it to join ties of relationship, or dealing with it in a right way, this man being in the worst station.

"4. A man whom Allah provides with neither property nor knowledge, who says that if he had property he would deal with it as so and so does and has this intention, the load they have to bear being equal."[39]

---

[39] *Sunan at-Tirmidhi*, Zuhd, 17; Ahmad ibn Hanbal, *Al-Musnad*, 4/231.

3. Benevolence Secures Social Peace

Extending a helping hand to the needy in the society is the best thing that can be done to warrant a peaceful future for the society. When we provide financial support to destitute people, we may be able to help them to refrain from illegal or illegitimate actions in which they may feel forced to engage out of despair. Benevolence protects the poor. By helping them to satisfy their material needs, we protect them from evil deeds. Indeed, poverty drags many weak-kneed people to evil deeds, such theft or unfairness.

In many *hadith*s, the Messenger of Allah, peace and blessings be upon him, indicates that a community cannot find peace as long as some of its members are unhappy or restless. Therefore, overall happiness of a community is dependent on the happiness of each member. Those who fail to spare a few bucks for charity today may be unable to avoid future social turmoil or chaos even if they are eager to spend thousands. So it is clear that peace and happiness of individuals is closely dependent on overall social peace and happiness.

Benevolence not only eliminates the gap between the rich and the poor, but also helps to create such a bond of affection and respect between them.

4. Benevolence Is Conducive to Competition in Virtue

"The upper (giving) hand is better than the lower (taking) hand," says the Prophet. Thus, he makes it clear that it is better for Muslims to be in the position of the giver than to be in the position of the taker. Those who receive financial support, understanding, and affection from their Muslims sisters or believers in times of hardship and straits will try to be in the position of donors after they recover from hardships. This will trigger competition in virtue in the society.

READING TEXT
Sharing Bread Is Sweeter than the Bread Itself
(Adapted from a *Hadith*)

The last lesson of the day had come to an end. The students were growing impatient to get out. They placed their books in their bags, prepared to leave as soon as the bell rang. Only Ali was unprepared and was doing everything in his power to be late. Finally, the bell rang and the students headed for the door at a stroke. Ali did not budge. He gathered his belongings slowly. Looking at his teacher with the corner of his eye on one hand, he was waiting for his friends to leave on the other. His teacher noticed his state and said,

"What's the matter, Ali? Aren't you going home?"

Seeing that his last friend had left, he answered,

"I wanted to speak with you, Miss."

"All right," his teacher said. "What is it that you wanted to speak to me about?"

"You know my friend Ahmet…"

"Yes, what happened to him?"

"Their situation isn't very good, I think. His mother doesn't seem to put good things in his lunchbox."

"And…"

"I want to help him, but he'll be upset if he finds out I'm helping him. What if I put aside a piece of *simit* each day and gave these to you at the end of the week and you gave these to him?"

He removed a handful of coins and placed them on his teacher's desk. Miss Nurhan did not touch the coins. She sat in her chair and began thinking. She went through everything she knew about Ali. As far as she was aware, his family's situation was not too good. How well meaning and thoughtful this hardworking and sweet student was. He was not the child of a wealthy family. Despite this, he wanted to help. What is more, he did not want this to be known.

Miss Nurhan said, "Hang on a minute, Ali. As far as I know, your family's financial situation is not very good either. Am I right?"

"You are right, Miss. My dad's a day laborer and he can't find work most of the time. But I'm working and earning money also."

"Where are you working?"

"I sell *simit*."

Miss Nurhan again paused to think. What should she now say in relation to so much kindness? It was difficult to make this happen. She had to find a way of talking him out of this, but without breaking the heart of her endearing student. If she spoke with him a little longer she could perhaps have found a way. Miss Nurhan turned to Ali and said,

"What do you want to be when you grow up?"

"A very wealthy businessman."

"Why?"

"To help people more."

"That's nice," she said. "Now look, Ali. Ahmet's family is not in a very good situation, this is true. But yours is not too different to his. If you like, don't rush. You can help people when you become very rich, can't you?"

"No," said Ali. "I must help now."

"Why?"

"For three reasons... The first: this money isn't mine anyway. Because I do good, Allah makes me liked by others. And this affects people, so they buy more *simit*. Because of this, I sell even more *simit* than those working the whole day. There is especially Uncle Hasan in our neighborhood, who buys two *simit*s each day and feeds it to the pigeons. Secondly, if I can't learn how to do good from now, then I won't be able to at all when I grow up. If I don't do acts of goodness now and leave them to when I'm rich, then I'll delay when I'm rich to the days when I become even richer and so fool myself. The third is even more important: When I grow up, I want to be a very rich businessman. Those who don't make investments at the right time can't be great businessmen."

Miss Nurhan listened as though she had an adult before her:

"I couldn't quite understand this last one," she said.

"Let me explain Miss," Ali said. "Because I'm not that rich right now, I can only help as much as a piece of *simit* each day. I can't give any more. Allah gives to those who do good to the best of their ability. Seeing that I am able now, then the price of Paradise is as much as a few pieces of *simit*. If I die without becoming rich, then I can enter Paradise with a few *simit* pieces. Can there be a more profitable investment than this?"

Tears welled in Miss Nurhan's eyes. Whilst nodding in agreement, she sent Ali off home.

When returning to the classroom, she realized that the school was completely empty and when she reached her desk, she noticed the coins that Ali had left were still on her desk. She sat on her chair without thinking and took the coins in her hand. No money had ever seemed this valuable to her before. It was as though she was holding the world's most precious pearls, rubies, and diamonds. These coins were even more valuable than those. These coins, this loose change was money that could purchase Paradise. She held these coins with the sense of never wanting to let them go. Miss Nurhan was unable to get up from where she sat. She felt her insides well up and felt herself engulfed by emotions impossible to describe. She began to weep, like a sudden heavy downpour of rain. She cried and cried.

When she collected herself, it had gotten dark. As she left the school with slow steps, Sadık the watchman heard Miss Nurhan repeating to herself, "Purchasing Paradise with loose change, purchasing Paradise with loose change." Not even hearing the watchman's saying in astonishment, "What did you say, Miss?" the teacher disappeared into the twilight under the watchman's perplexed gaze.

Indeed, when you look around you, you will see a great many Ali's and Ayşe's. What we are charged with is to see to their needs. Even if our financial situation is not good, sharing even a piece of bread holds great merit. Don't forget, sharing bread is sweeter than the bread itself.

Compete with One Another in Kindness!

With respect to the commands and recommendations in both the Qur'an and the traditions of the noble Prophet, each of the Companions virtually competed with one another in kindness and generosity, raced to help others with enthusiasm, and strived to perform acts of kindness. Indeed, nothing less could possibly have been expected from these sincere individuals whose path was constantly enlightened by the kindling flame of faith they bore in their hearts. If we expect any kind of movement in terms of charity and kindness in our social lives, then as in every aspect, we should follow in the footsteps of the Companions and raise generations of generosity and kindness. Witnessing this in the various charity organizations established in different places and times is certainly a source of hope for the future. The examples of kindness and generosity that are very few today were spread among the public by the Companions who displayed outstanding effort, saying, "People who compete with each other should do so in kindness and charity."

This Golden Generation, those who shed tears because they we unable to participate in a campaign due to poverty—and were mentioned in a verse of the Qur'an—competed with one another in spreading generosity and kindness. The noble Prophet responded to the poor Companions who said they were unable to attain the status the wealthy had achieved, being therefore deprived of reward, by advising them how to attain a reward of equal status and telling them that this was a Divine favor. Abu Hurayra related this event:

> Some of the poor Muhajirun (Migrants) came to the noble Prophet and said, "The wealthy people will gain higher status and will have permanent enjoyment, but they pray like us and fast as we do."
>
> When the Messenger of Allah asked why, they replied, "They have more money by which they perform the *Hajj*, and *Umra*; to strive in Allah's Cause and give in charity."
>
> The noble Prophet said, "Shall I not tell you a thing, which if enacted, would enable you to catch up with those who have surpassed you? Nobody would overtake you, and you would be better than the people amongst whom you live, except those who would do the same. Say *Subhanallah* (Glory be to Allah), *Alhamdulillah* (All praise be to Allah) and *Allahu Akbar* (Allah is great) thirty-three times after every compulsory Prayer."
>
> Then after a while they returned and said, "The rich have heard what you told us to do and are doing the same."
>
> The Messenger of Allah replied, "This is a favor of Allah, and He gives it to whom He wishes."

Nevertheless, in other traditions the Messenger of Allah consoled these Companions by guiding them as to how they could earn reward. According to the tidings he gave regarding this subject, if the poor ones who admire the rich ones—those who spend their wealth on the path of Allah—say with sincerity, *If only I had wealth, I would also dis-*

tribute it as so and so gives in charity and spend it on the path of Allah, they would also attain the same reward. In terms of sincerity and good intention, there is no distinction between the one who gives a percentage of what little he possesses and a rich person giving the same percentage. In addition to pointing out the atmosphere of generosity prevailed over the Companions in general, it will suffice to convey this famous tradition relating the competition between Abu Bakr and Umar in spending on the path of Allah. As Umar relates, "One day, the Messenger of Allah ordered us to give charity; this coincided with a time that I had possessions. I thought to myself, *I will exceed him in giving charity today if I will at any time*. So I took half of my wealth to the Messenger of Allah.

Abu Bakr asked me, "What have you left for your family?"

I replied, "An equal amount."

Then Abu Bakr brought all of his possessions. The Messenger of Allah asked him the same question and he replied, "I have left Allah and His Messenger for them."

At that moment, I realized that I would never be able to compete with him in giving charity."

This is what they considered giving charity, and by continuing this throughout their lives, they attained the pleasure of Allah.

What Are the Principles That Should Be Respected in Spending in Charity?

We have mentioned it above: Benevolence is an important deed that increases one's esteem both in the eyes of Allah and the general public. In performing this important deed, there are of course principles we need to pay respect to. Otherwise, our benevolent deeds may not produce the desired results if done without respecting these principles.

We need to pay close attention to the following principles in particular:

1. Charity is essentially performed only to seek the good pleasure of Allah. Any benevolent deed is not acceptable to Allah if done without seeking the pleasure of Allah. The benevolent deeds done for show or ostentation or for gaining certain advantages through them fall into this category.

In the Holy Qur'an, our Lord cautions us:

> (O people,) whatever good you spend (in charity and other good causes) is to your own benefit, and (as believers) you do not spend but in search of Allah's 'Face' (seeking to be worthy of His approval). Whatever good you spend will be repaid to you in full, and you will not be wronged. (Al-Baqarah 2:272).

2. We need to be picky about those to whom we pay our charity and we should diligently try to find out if they really need our help. Many people tend to have ill-gotten gains by playing on other people's heartstrings and begging although they are not really poor. On the other hand, many destitute people are so ashamed of begging something from other people that they just keep silent and wait for someone to extend a helping hand to them.

Allah the Almighty commands:

> That (which you spend) is for the poor who, having dedicated themselves to Allah's cause, are in distressed circumstances. They are unable to move about the earth (to render service in Allah's cause and earn their livelihood). Those who are unaware (of their circumstances) suppose them wealthy because of their abstinence and dignified bearing, but you will know them by their countenance—they do not beg of people importunately. And whatever good you spend, surely Allah has full knowledge of it. (Al-Baqarah 2:273).

3. We should not give the useless things which we no longer want to use to other as charity. In other words, we should try to empathize with the people whom we seek to help, and imagine what we would feel if we were given the same thing as charity. Therefore, we should refrain from giving people the things whose quality or quantity would be unacceptable to ourselves if the same things were given to us. In this context, the Holy Qur'an cautions us:

> O you who believe! Spend (in Allah's cause and for the needy) out of the pure, wholesome things you have earned and of what We have produced for you from the earth, and do not seek after the bad things to spend thereof (in alms and in Allah's cause) when you would not take it save with disdain; and know that Allah is All-Wealthy and Self-Sufficient (absolutely independent of the charity

of people), All-Praiseworthy (as your Lord, Who provides for you
and all other beings and meets all your needs). (Al-Baqarah 2:267).

The following *hadith* is very thought-provoking:

In the Age of Happiness, some people would bring date bunches
to the Prophet's Mosque so that poor people may take them. One day,
the Messenger of Allah entered the mosque and saw some poor quality bunches. Pointing at them with his staff, he said: "The person who
brought this sadaqa could have brought better quality sadaqa. He will
get the poor quality reception on the Day of Judgment."[40]

4. We should never recount our benevolent deeds or put other under
obligation or taunt them. Almsgiving done in this way is not beneficial
to the almsgiver. In the Holy Qur'an, Allah the Almighty refers to such
deeds as acts by unbelievers:

> O you who believe! Render not vain your almsgiving by putting (the
> receiver) under an obligation and taunting—like him who spends his
> wealth to show off to people and be praised by them, and believes
> not in Allah and the Last Day. The parable of his spending is that
> of a rock on which there is soil; a heavy rain falls upon it, and leaves
> it barren. They have no power (control) over what they have earned.
> Allah guides not such disbelieving people (to attain their goals).
> (Al-Baqarah 2:264).

5. The quantity of benevolence does not matter. We should not be
stopped by the fact that we can give only small amounts of alms. But
we should try to do our best in helping others at the highest level. In
this context, our Prophet, peace and blessings be upon him, says, "Do
not scorn any kindness even if it consists of smiling at your brother."[41]

6. We should not postpone our benevolent deeds. It is wrong to
delay our aids to other people with various considerations. Instead, we
should waste no time in helping the needy within our capabilities.

7. Performing our benevolent deeds in secrecy, except for prescribed
purifying alms (*zakah*) is a must. Indeed, *zakah* is an obligatory act of
worship, and openness is essential in such acts. However, we must stick

---

[40] *Sunan Abu Dawud*, Zakah, 17.
[41] *Riyadh as-Salihin, 1:159.*

to the principle of secrecy while giving alms to the needy for fear of hypocrisy. In this regard, our Lord says, *"If you conceal it and give it to the poor (in secret), this is better for you; and Allah will (make it an atonement to) blot out some of your evil deeds"* (al-Baqarah 2:271).

In a *hadith*, our Prophet, peace and blessings be upon him, explains that those who donate their alms in such a way that the left hand does not know what the right hand gives will be shaded by Allah under His shade on the day when there will be no shade except His.[42]

So far, we have listed the principles for the people who give alms. Receivers of alms should refrain from taking beyond what really need. They should remember that there may be other people who really need what they don't really need. Also, they should not scorn the alms finding it too little. Instead, they should thank and pray for the almsgiver.

QUESTIONS

1. What should we do to "attain godliness and virtue" with what we spend in charity or good causes?
   a. To spend of what we love
   b. To give things we find useless or don't use
   c. To donate things that are unneeded or of poor quality
   d. None of the above

2. What is the prerequisite, stated in *hadiths*, for Allah to help His servant?
   a. The servant performs his/her own tasks
   b. The servant helps other people
   c. The servant performs his/her tasks regularly
   d. The servant performs his/her task in a timely manner

3. Which of the following is not related to the concept of benevolence?
   a. *Sadaqa* (alms)
   b. *Zakah* (Prescribed Purifying Alms)
   c. *Qard al-hasan* (good loan)
   d. *Tayammum*

---

[42] *Tajrid*, 2:620.

4. Which form of helpfulness is disapproved?

    a. Helping each other in good deeds

    b. Helping each other in refraining from evil deeds

    c. Helping each other in hostility and sins

    d. Helping friends with their needs

5. Which Companion donated his beloved garden named Bayruha in Allah's cause?

    a. Anas ibn Malik   b. Abu Talha

    c. Abu Aqil   d. Abdurrahman ibn Awf

6. Who is the Companion who became a paragon of "spending in Allah's cause" by giving the poor and our Prophet the money he earned by working as a porter?

    a. Abu Aqil   b. Abu Talha

    c. Abdurrahman ibn Awf   d. Abu Bakr

7. Which of the following is the Companion who spent his entire wealth in Allah's cause and when the Prophet asked, "What did he left behind?" said, "Allah and His Messenger"?

    a. Umar   b. Abu Bakr

    c. Abdurrahman ibn Awf   d. Abu Dhar

8. What does the *hadith*, "Do not scorn any kindness even if it consists of smiling at your brother," mean?

    a. We should not consider any charity as too little

    b. We should not postpone our benevolent deeds

    c. We should give alms in secrecy

    d. We should make sure our alms should go to the needy

9. Which of the following is related to the concept of benevolence?

    a. Altruism (selflessness)   b. Self-sacrifice

    c. *Infaq* and munificence   d. All of the above

10. Who is the Companion who owned money only to pay for his needs for two days and to whom Umar said, "This world has changed all of us except you"?

    a. Abu Dhar   b. Abu Ubayda

    c. Hudhayfa ibn al-Yaman   d. Muadh ibn Jabal

5.

TRUTHFULNESS, HONESTY, VERACITY, AND KEEPING PROMISES

"One cannot have the proper faith if his heart is not righteous. His heart cannot become righteous if he does not tell the truth. The one from whose evil his neighbor does not feel safe will not enter Paradise." (Ahmad ibn Hanbal, *Al-Musnad*, 3/198).

What Is Loyalty?

Loyalty means truthfulness, keeping one's promises and integrity. Loyalty also means asking for goodness of one's sisters or brothers in religion for the sake of Allah, being kindly toward them, camaraderie, keeping agreements, keeping promises, preserving what is entrusted, and performing assigned tasks. The antonym of loyalty is betrayal.

Betrayal does not befit a mature Muslim. In the affairs among themselves or with other people, Muslims must stick to the principles of loyalty, integrity and honesty. The antonym of integrity is dishonesty.

Integrity occurs at the verbal, intellectual, and behavioral levels. Believers will always stand on the principles of integrity and honesty. The Holy Qur'an clearly puts integrity and straightforwardness in the spotlight. Allah the Almighty commands: "*O you who believe! Act in reverence for Allah and piously, without doing anything to incur His punishment, and always speak words true, proper, and straight to the point*" (al-Ahzab 33:70). This verse underlines that a believer must be honest at all times.

In the following sections, we will study all aspects of loyalty (to truth) in detail.

What Is the Straight Path? Who Is the Truthful Person?

Truthfulness is a concept that comprises all moral qualities. We need to understand what the Straight Path is in order to make sense of this concept. So what is the Straight Path? Every day we recite the Al-Fatiha at least 40 times in our Prayers. *"Guide us to the Straight Path, The Path of those whom You have favored, not of those who have incurred (Your) wrath (punishment and condemnation), nor of those who are astray,"* (al-Fatiha, 1:6–7) we say, to ask from Allah our guidance to the Straight Path.

These verses make it clear that the Straight Path is the way of the Prophets Allah sent as guides to people. For us, the Straight Path is the way of our Prophet, i.e., the Islam's way. A truthful person is the one who obeys Allah's commandments, leads a life to the pleasure of Allah and respects the rights of other people.

As the Straight Path is the way of our Prophet, the most truthful person is necessarily our Prophet. Therefore, a believer who wants to be truthful should take our Prophet's morals as a model.

Our Beloved Prophet Was "Trustworthy"

The Quraysh were repairing the Ka'ba. They had a division of labor among themselves. In this way, every tribe could enjoy the honor of the repair of the Ka'ba. The construction work had finally finished. Now, Hajar al-Aswad (Holy Black Stone) would be placed into its place. Every tribe wanted to have this honor by performing this task. Therefore, a debate had erupted among them and they had even come closer to killing each other. A bloody clash was only a matter of time.

Then, Abu Umayya ibn al-Mughira, the oldest man in the Quraysh, made the following proposal: "Let us make the first man to enter from the gate of Safa our umpire. Let us as accept what he tells us to do."

Everyone accepted this reasonable proposal. It was morning. Everyone was waiting intently for the first man to enter. When they saw Prophet Muhammad, peace and blessings be upon him, enter, they all rejoiced. This was because everyone knew him as a truthful and honest. Already, they used to refer to him as "al-Amin" (the trusted, truthful and loyal one).

They explained the matter to our Prophet. The Messenger of Allah wants to ensure everyone's involvement in this great honor. He wanted them to bring a cloak. Then, he put Hajar al-Aswad on the cloak. He asked each tribe leader to hold one end of the clock and lift it together. Thus, every tribe had its share from the honor of carrying Hajar al-Aswad to its destination. Then, he took Hajar al-Aswad and placed it at its position.

He had become a Prophet at the age of 40, but the decent life he had led until that age seemed to lay the groundwork for his Prophethood. He was truthful, loyal, and reliable, both before and after he became a Prophet. There was no room for dishonesty in his life.

Here is an example. Mughira ibn Shu'ba, a Companion of the Prophet, narrates: At that time, I had not been blessed with Islam yet. I was walking with Abu Jahl. At one point, we came across to the Prophet. We were in a state of extreme frivolity. He came to us with dignity and manners that you would expect from him. He explained us the truth. Abu Jahl said to him: "If we had accepted your Prophethood, we would already have been converted to your religion and followed you. But we don't recognize you as such." Hearing these words, the Prophet left us alone. Then, Abu Jahl said to me: "Actually, everything he said is true. He doesn't tell lies. We have never seen him tell a lie. But I cannot bear it if the Children of Abdul-Muttalib boast saying: 'We have already had the honor of distributing water to pilgrims, protecting the Ka'ba and serving food to pilgrims. Now, we have the honor of having a Prophet.'"

This is a significant confession that shows us that the truthfulness of the Prophet had made a great impact on people. Having read and studied the qualifications of our Prophet in the Torah and seeing the face of our Prophet, Abdullah ibn Salam said, "By Allah, this face is not that of an impostor," and he became a Muslim saying, "There is no deity but Allah, and Muhammad is His Messenger."

A man who had later become a Companion narrates: In the Age of Ignorance (Jahiliyya), I had made an appointment with the Prophet. I forgot about my promise. Three days later, I remembered it, and rushed to our meeting place. I saw that the Messenger of Allah was there. He was not angry with me. He just said: "O young man, you put me to inconvenience. I have been waiting for you here for three days."

Here is another example: Ammar, the son of Yasir and Sumayya, who was one of the first martyrs of Islam, came home. "Where were you, son?" his parents asked. "I was with the Messenger of Allah," Ammar replied. "Is he a Prophet?" they asked. "Yes," said their son, "He talks about Allah and the Book."

Then, the father spoke: "Muhammad is a trustworthy person who did not tell a single lie. A person who does not tell lies to people cannot tell lies about Allah," and he immediately became a Muslim.

We continue to discuss the truthful and loyal life of our Prophet, peace and blessings be upon him. The Messenger of Allah used to make jokes from time to time. But even his jokes would stick to truthfulness. When our Companions would make jokes using statements which were contrary to facts or truth, our Prophet cautioned them not to do so. Indeed, a believer should be truthful in his words even if he is joking. Dishonesty is closer to disbelief than belief. A person who tells a lie takes a step closer to disbelief. One does not become an unbeliever by telling a lie, but dishonesty is a sign of hypocrisy.

Indeed, falsity kills humor. In this context, our Prophet constitutes a good example. For instance, he would summon Anas, who had been serving him since the age of 10 or 11, by saying, "Ya dhal udhu-nayn" (O two-eared one). This is truthfulness. Yet calling someone two-eared may express a different meaning based on the situation. Here, our Prophet told the truth. He knew how to be true even while joking.

Once, an old woman came to visit him. The Messenger of Allah saw her innocence and her bright face and gladdened her with his witty remarks. When the woman talked about her desire concerning Paradise, the Prince of Prophets said, "The elderly cannot enter Paradise." The woman started to cry, and the Prophet said, "Tell her that she won't enter Paradise as an old woman."

In this joke, the Prophet created a mental tension before uttering his final remark. His jokes never contained false information. He always told the truth.

The Supporter of the Truthful Is Allah the Almighty

Truthfulness is keeping in mind the benefits of others, bringing them correct information. Being truthful means telling the truth, thinking in the right way, and behaving in the right way. In everything one must say what is right, and even if it is against his own interest or the interest of his relatives.

The sense of confidence provided by being truthful prevents relationships between members of a society from going sour, and prevents solidarity from fading away. The truthful person never contradicts himself. In short, all the psycho-social problems born out of lying are prevented. Truthfulness brings inner peace to all people, and especially to the hearts of the believers. This is because Allah, may His glory be exalted, supports the truthful ones.

A story further illustrates this truth. There was an oppressive governor in the city where Hasan al-Basri used to live. One day, the governor sent his henchmen to apprehend Hasan al-Basri, hoping he would be harmful to him and his cause. In turn, Hasan took refuge in the hut of Habib al-Ajami, with whom he taught for a while in the past. A henchman came in a rage and said:

"Have you seen Hasan al-Basri?"

"Yes."

"Where?"

"Here in my hut."

The men enter the hut. Somehow they cannot find him there. When they come out, they ask again, even more angrily:

"O sheikh, why are telling lies?"

"I have not lied. If you did not see him, what crime did I commit?"

So again they searched the hut. And again they did not find him. When they left, Hasan al-Basri said: "O Habib! I know that, for your sake, my Lord did not show me to them. But why did you tell them about my place? Didn't I have a right of teaching over you?"

Embarrassed, Habib uttered these profound words: "O my teacher! The reason they were not able to find you was not me, but your truthfulness. You know that Allah is the supporter of the truthful. If I told them a lie, they would have taken both of us."

A believer keeps his word, does not betray any trust, does what he must do, fulfills the tasks he shoulders, and gives leadership positions to trustworthy ones. He demonstrates the profound and complete ethics of trustworthiness in his worship and obedience. He is tied to his Lord from the bottom of his heart. He would never venture to be insincere to Him. He would never worship others, and does not cheat in his devotions.

The Holy Qur'an Enjoins Truthfulness

Upon telling a lie, a mature person will experience bad conscience based on his faith. Truthfulness saves us from experiencing such paradoxes and uneasiness. In this context, our Prophet says, "Truthfulness leads to calmness (peace of heart) while lies to suspicion and hesitation."[43] Truthfulness is a key characteristic that paves the way to other moral virtues and urges people to stick to moral values. "Truthfulness leads one to goodness," our beloved Prophet says.[44]

"Promise me to do the following six things and I will promise you Paradise:

1. Speak the truth when you speak!
2. Keep your promise!
3. Be trustworthy in regard of what is entrusted to you!
4. Guard your modesty!
5. Do not look at what is forbidden to see!
6. Do not bother people physically or verbally."[45]

Loyal people keep their promises. They wear their hearts on their sleeves. They don't lie; they don't cheat anyone; they don't deceive anyone; they do their jobs properly. They follow the straight path. A believer should be loyal and truthful first in essence (in his heart). He shouldn't allow dishonesty, lies, deception, hostility, or sedition to dwell in his

---

[43] *Sunan at-Tirmidhi*, Qiyamah, 60.
[44] *Sahih Muslim*, Birr, 105; *Sahih al-Bukhari*, Adab, 69.
[45] *Al-Musnad*, 5/323.

heart. He should speak the truth. He should refrain from resorting to lies, deception or slander while speaking. The harms of dishonesty are obvious while the benefits of truthfulness are many. A believer should then be loyal and truthful with regard to his job. He should do his job properly, keeping away from deception and cheating.

A person who is truthful and who is a paragon of truthfulness and who accepts the Divine revelation without hesitation is called as "siddiq" (loyal and truthful). Indeed, Siddiq was the honorific title of Abu Bakr. Siddiq people never lie. They are straightforward with their beliefs and confirm this with their actions. *"And make mention of Abraham in the Book. He was surely a sincere man of truth, a Prophet"* (Maryam, 19:41). *"Those who believe in Allah and His Messengers (those whose actions prove their profession of faith)—they are, in the sight of their Lord, the loyal and truthful (to Allah, in whatever they do and say), and the witnesses (who have borne testimony to the truth with their lives)"* (al-Hadid 57:19).

In the Holy Qur'an, Allah calls all people to *"keep the company of the truthful (those who are also faithful to their covenant with Allah)"* (at-Tawbah 9:119). Allah will reward the truthful ones who are loyal to Islam, the Qur'an, and the blessed Prophet. He will punish the hypocrites who are not truthful.[46]

Allah has prepared forgiveness (to bring unforeseen blessings) and a tremendous reward for all truly believing men and truly believing women as they are honest and truthful in their speech and true to their words in their actions.[47] Believers are *sadiqs* (friends) with truthfulness. They testify a true call from Allah and they became *musaddiq* (testifiers) and truthful. Our Lord praises them in the following verses:

> Whoever obeys Allah and the Messenger (as they must be obeyed), then those are (and in the Hereafter will be, in Paradise) in the company of those whom Allah has favored (with the perfect guidance)—the Prophets, and the truthful ones (loyal to Allah's cause and truthful in whatever they do and say), and the witnesses (those who see the hidden Divine truths and testify thereto with their lives), and the righteous ones (in all their deeds and sayings, and dedicated

---

46 Al-Ahzab 33:24.

47 Al-Ahzab 33:35.

to setting everything right). How excellent they are for companions! (An-Nisa 4:69).

Sadiq means a friend. In other words, *sadiq* is a confidant who affirms
his friend and who treats him in the correct manner and who is loyal
to his friend. It is quite interesting that this word is etymologically derived
from the word "sidq," which means "truthfulness."

READING TEXT
Truthfulness, Lies and Vain Speech

Foreigners living in Turkey for various reasons are in consensus on one
thing: They state that when they do business with a Turkish Muslim,
there is no need for a contract and that one's word is enough. This situation is a natural outcome of the Turkish Islamic ethics and morality.
Muslims possessing the morals of the Qur'an are described in the
Qur'anic verse entitled Baqarah with the words, "*And those (are godly
and virtuous) who fulfill their covenant when they have engaged in a covenant*" (al-Baqarah 2:177). In the continuation of the verse, it is stated,
"Those are they who are true (in their faith), and those are they who have
achieved righteousness, piety, and due reverence for Allah."

French general Comte de Bonneval expressed his admiration for the
honesty of the Turks saying, "Such crimes as injustice, monopolism,
and theft are virtually unknown among Turks. In short, whether born
of a belief of conscience or a fear of punishment, they display such a
degree of integrity that many a time a person finds themselves struck
with admiration for the honesty of the Turks."

The fastidiousness of a Turkish merchant regarding honesty is presented in the following: Upon a foreign textile merchant's coming to
the Ottoman lands and wanting to buy all the fabric of a particular
fabric manufacturer whose product he was pleased with, he noticed the
owner put aside a roll of fabric when balancing up the rolls. When he
inquired after the reason, the Ottoman merchant said, "I can't give this
to you, it's faulty."

Despite the foreign merchant's saying, "No harm done. It's no problem," the Ottoman merchant insisted upon not selling that roll of fabric

and said, "I have told you that these goods are faulty and you are aware of this. But when you sell this in your own country, your customers are not going to know that I told you all this. Thus, I would have sold your customers faulty goods. Ottoman pride, honor and dignity will be offended and they will think us deceitful. This is why I cannot give you this faulty roll under any circumstances." This is how he explained his reason for not selling this roll of fabric.

One of the characteristics differentiating the Turks from other nations is deception and falsehood being unknown to them. The religion of Islam has enabled the Turks to adopt good moral qualities and reject the corrupt. This point is related in a nineteenth century source as follows: "It is in the middle rank of life, among men subsisting by their own industry, and equally removed from poverty and riches, that we must look for the national character: and among the Turks of this class, the domestic and social virtues are united with knowledge adequate to their wants, and with patriarchal urbanity of manners. Honesty is the characteristic of the Turkish merchant... In the Turkish villages, where there is no mixture of Greeks, innocence of life and simplicity of manners are conspicuous, and roguery and deceit are unknown." (Thomas Thornton (1762–1814), a British merchant in the Near East and writer on Turkey).

French merchant traveler Du Loir's observations in the seventeenth-century serve as a clear summary: "Undoubtedly, Turkish politics and civilized life, with respect to morality, is in a position to serve as a model for the entire world."

The Muslim Is Honest and Trustworthy

A Muslim is a person who is honest and trustworthy and whose speech and actions to not contradict their thought and feeling. They take great pains to ensure and maintain such a state. The Messenger of Allah paid special attention to the establishment of this moral principle in childhood. In view of preventing parents from falling into the error of lying to their children, he established certain general principles guiding the parent-child relationship.

For instance, it is unacceptable for parents to deceive their children, under any circumstances, and for them to assume an air of indifference in their treatment and relationship with their children. Abdullah ibn Amir relates: "My mother called me one day when the Messenger of Allah was sitting in our house. She said: Come here and I shall give you something. The Messenger of Allah asked her: What did you intend to give him? She replied: I intended to give him some dates. The Messenger of Allah said: If you were not to give him anything, a lie would be recorded against you."[48]

Abu Hurayra also relates a similar narration: "Allah's Messenger said, 'Whoever says to a child, "Come here, I will give you something," and then does not give them anything will be accountable for lying.'"[49]

A Muslim's inner conformity to his or her outer appearance is also critical for integrity. Just as we are to refrain from harmful words, so too must we restrain ourselves from hateful feelings or thoughts. In other words, a Muslim should speak as they think, and act according to their word; there should be no difference between who they are inside and who they appear to be. The following *hadith* addresses this aspect of integrity: "A person whose heart is not correct cannot have correct faith. If the tongue does not speak truth, the heart cannot be right, and if the person's neighbors are not safe from him, he cannot enter Paradise" (*Al-Musnad*, 3/198). Here the Prophet teaches that the heart and the tongue should be consistent with each other, and both of them should manifest integrity.

When there is consistency between a Muslim's inner self and outer actions, they will always be honest, both at work and in business. A Muslim must be careful never to cheat or deceive others to gain greater profit or for any other reason.

A *hadith* handed down by Abu Hurayra reports, "One day the Prophet saw (a man selling) a heap of wheat. He put his hand into the pile and found that, while the top was dry, the bottom was damp. He asked the seller, 'What is this?' The man said, 'The rain wet it.' The Prophet

---

[48] *Sunan Abu Dawud*, Adab, 219.
[49] *Al-Musnad*, 2/452.

responded, 'You should put the wet part on top (so people can see it). One who cheats us is not of us.'"

Abu Said al-Khudri narrated that the Messenger of Allah said, "Traders who do not swerve from uprightness and trustworthiness will be together with the Prophets, the truthful, the martyrs and the righteous."[50]

One of the most unique characteristics of the blessed Companions of the Prophet—perhaps their most important characteristic—was their unfailing integrity and righteousness. These qualities brought a deep atmosphere of peace and security to their inner lives as well as to their interpersonal relations.

Once Abu al-Hawra asked Hasan ibn Ali, "What have you memorized from Allah's Messenger?" He answered, "What did you memorize from the Messenger of Allah?" He said: "I memorized from him: 'Leave that which makes you doubt for that which does not make you doubt.'"[51] In a similar narration, Sufyan ibn Abdullah al-Sakafi said, "O Messenger of Allah, give me such knowledge of Islam that it will suffice me and I will never need to ask anyone else about Islam." He answered, "Say, 'I believe in Allah,' and then be completely honest in everything."[52]

READING TEXT
What Do Saintly Servants of Allah Think about Truthfulness?

Let us hearken to the advice from the paragons of spirituality about the significance of truthfulness:

Truthfulness is something that is entrusted to us. Lying is disloyalty to that trust. (Abu Bakr as-Siddiq).

Son, keep away from dishonesty, which is sweet like the sparrow meat. Few people can get rid of it. (Luqman the Wise).

The biggest mistake before Allah is to tell lies. (Ali ibn Abi Talib).

Liars and parsimonious people will enter Hell. But I don't know which group will go deeper into the pit. (Sha'bi).

---

50 *Sunan at-Tirmidhi*, Buyu, 4.
51 *Sunan an-Nasa'i*, Book 51, Hadith 173.
52 *Sahih Muslim*, Iman, 62.

Truth and dishonesty wrestle with each other until one removes the other from the heart. (Malik Deenar).

Hypocrisy is the source of discord between inner feelings and outer actions. And dishonesty is the source of hypocrisy. (Hasan al-Basri).

The venerable Companions of the Prophet wouldn't loathe anything as they would loathe dishonesty as they believed belief cannot coexist with dishonesty. (Aisha bint Abu Bakr).

Straightforwardness is superior to extraordinary Divine favors. (Sayyid Abdulhakim Arwasi).

People asked Luqman, "How did you attain this station?" He replied, "By sticking to truthfulness, safeguarding the trusts, and abandoning what I don't need."

People asked Sheik Abdu'l-Qadir al-Jilani: "What was your basis when you first started? Which deed helped you to attain such a high station?" He replied: "My basis was truthfulness. I never lied. My heart was always on my sleeve. Thanks to this, I was successful."

The best deed is truthfulness and the worst one is dishonesty.

The one who says, "I never see a truthful person," would find the truthful people if he himself were a truthful man.

Islam has three pillars: truth, loyalty, and justice. When a person combines three qualities, he is certainly a righteous person. These are: refraining from carnal desires, being truthful for the sake of Allah, and eating religiously permissible and clean food. (Sayyid Abdulhakim Arwasi).

A Loyal Person Can Keep Secrets

A secret told to a person is like something entrusted to him. A loyal person can be trusted to keep that secret. He won't disclose any secret entrusted to him. He won't share it with others. He knows closely the meaning the saying, "The secret is your slave, but you become its slave if you disclose it."

As Ali put it, keeping a secret is a test of one's willpower. If a person cannot pass this test, he won't be successful in life. A truthful person knows that he must keep any secret that is entrusted to him or he will run into irreversible complications.

While some secrets may be personal, others may concern the family, the country, the cause, the nation or companies. Our Prophet attached great importance to keeping secrets and gave them advice about the importance of keeping secrets. Let us give an example:

Abdullah ibn Jafar narrates: "One day, the Messenger of Allah took me to the back of his mount and said something to me as a secret. I cannot tell it to anyone."[53]

Once Anas ibn Malik, who was serving the Prophet, was late to come home. "Why are you late?" asked his mother. "The Messenger of Allah had sent me for an errand," he replied. "What was it about?" asked his mother. "It is a secret," Anas replied. Being an insightful, intelligent, and prudent woman, his mother said, "Then, don't tell the Prophet's secrets to anyone." Her attitude should be taken as model by parents in teaching the importance of keeping secrets to their children.[54]

Now, let us have a look at what Fethullah Gülen said about keeping secrets:

Secret is like an irresistible power or an invincible army. Guarding a secret is the same as guarding one's chastity. Those who keep a secret, whether personal or a friend's, keep themselves chaste. Conversely, those who spread secrets damage their honor and reputation by leaving them unguarded. There are some states that must be kept secret as the person who has them will enjoy Divine favors as long as they are kept secret.

If you want to tell someone a secret, be sure that you could trust him or her with your honor. He or she must be as meticulous about keeping your secret as he or she would be about his or her own honor. An unreliable person, one who is ignorant of the value of chastity, should not be entrusted with keeping your secret.

Keeping a secret and respecting the secrets of others, as opposed to prying into them, is a virtue related to self-discipline and sensitivity. Those who lack understanding cannot guard a secret, and those who do not

---

53 *Sahih Muslim*, Haydh 79; *Sunan Abu Dawud*, Jihad, 44; *Sunan ibn Majah*, Taharah, 23; *Al-Darimi*, Wudu, 5; Ahmad ibn Hanbal, *Al-Musnad*, 1/204.

54 *Sahih al-Bukhari*, Istizan, 46; *Sahih Muslim*, Fadai'l as-Sahaba, 145 (2482).

care about the consequences of words and actions cannot be considered discreet.

If you entrust another secret to someone who previously disclosed one, your lack of perception and poor judgment in choosing a confidant is plain for all to see. One whose own heart is firm on this matter and who is vigilant cannot be deceived and seduced repeatedly in this way.

Explain what you must, but never give away all of your secrets. Those who freely publicize the secrets of their hearts drag themselves and their nation toward an inevitable downfall.

One should be very careful not to publicize his secrets. Especially, if they are some unpleasant, unlovable, and futile matters... Indeed, this may lead to inappropriate situations which may make our friends feel ashamed and our enemies feel happy.

Hearts are created as safes for keeping secrets. Intelligence is their lock; willpower is their key. No one can break into the safe and steal its valuables if the lock or key are not faulty.

Bear in mind that those who carry others' secrets to you might bear yours to others. Do not give such tactless people any chance to learn even the smallest details of your private concerns.

There are secrets related to the person, the family, and the nation. By disclosing a personal secret, you are interfering with a person's honor; by disclosing a family secret, you are interfering with the family's honor; and by disclosing a national secret, you are interfering with the nation's honor. A secret is a power only as long as it stays with its owner, but is a weapon that may be used against its owner if it passes into the hands of others. This is the meaning of one of our traditional sayings: "The secret is your slave, but you become its slave if you disclose it."

The details of many important affairs can be protected only if they are kept secret. Often enough, when the involved parties do not keep certain matters secret, no progress is achieved. In addition, serious risks might confront those who are involved, particularly if the matter concerns delicate issues of national life and its continuation.[55]

---

55   Gülen, M. Fethullah, *Sızıntı*, March 1983, 5:50.

Why Is Lying a Cardinal Sin?

Islam considers lying or dishonesty as one of major sins. "Shall I tell you the worst of cardinal sins?" our Prophet asked and repeated the question for three times. "Yes," our Companions replied. "Associating partners with Allah, failing to respect the rights of parents, and killing someone." Then, he added, "Beware of lies and false testimony." Thus, the Messenger of Allah listed dishonesty as a cardinal sin.[56]

Why is dishonesty considered a major sin? This is because dishonesty has the potential to trigger many other major sins. In comparison, other major sins are unrelated sins. However, dishonesty is associated with all of other major sins. For instance, when a person commits the major sin of drinking alcoholic drinks, he is prepared to tell a lie. A person who gambles may resort to lies in order to get back what he has lost.

Examples can be multiplied. In the Holy Qur'an, our Lord warns us about this obnoxious sin, saying, *"Shun all words of falsehood"* (al-Hajj 22:30) and *"O you who believe! Act in reverence for Allah and piously, without doing anything to incur His punishment, and always speak words true, proper and straight to the point"* (al-Ahzab 33:70). "For lying is the basis of unbelief; indeed, unbelief is a falsehood and the worst sort of lying, and it is the chief sign of dissembling. Lying is to slander Divine power and it is the opposite of dominical wisdom. Lying destroys high morals. It transforms great enterprises into putrefying corpses. Its poison has spread through the Islamic world. It has overturned the affairs of mankind, held back the world of humanity from attaining its perfections, and prevented its advance and progress."[57]

Lying is evil, big or small. A lie is a lie. There is no such thing as a white lie. One white lie leads to another and over time, dishonesty becomes part of our character. One concession breeds another. We may look down on little lies, but if we start to tell them, this may make into a habit.

---

[56] *Sahih al-Bukhari*, Shahadah, 10; *Sahih Muslim*, Iman, 143.
[57] Nursi, Bediüzzaman Said, *İşaratü'l-İ'caz* (Signs of Miraculousness), İstanbul: Şahdamar, 2010, p. 93.

Eventually, we start to tell bigger lies and we will be regarded as a liar in the eyes of Allah.

In a *hadith*, our beloved Prophet makes this case as follows:

"Beware of lies. Lying leads to sins, which, in turn, lead to Hell. If a person keeps telling lies and strives to tell lies, he is registered as a liar in Allah's sight."[58]

For this reason, a believer should be extremely careful about the truthfulness of his/her statements and alert against lies. How? Let us have a look at what Fethullah Gülen says about this matter. Gülen's position is as follows:

"Suppose there is a red carpet in front of us. Referring to it as a 'blue' carpet while speaking is clearly a lie as our statement does not conform to the facts. Suppose it is three minutes to nine. Someone asked you the time. You said, 'It is nine o'clock,' and it is a lie. The best thing to do is to tell exactly what the time is. There are some statements which are considered a hidden lie. For instance, suppose we are telling something in order to motivate people for benevolent or charity work. If we exaggerate our statements, it is an overstatement and a tacit or hidden lie. Such overstatements or lies may incur Divine action and we may end up losing the Divine assistance with that work. Moreover, spirits and spiritual ones may suffer from it. Our spiritual life may wither away. If a person is able to tell a lie even of this kind, there is a sign of hypocrisy in that person."[59]

Lying Is the Primary Sign of Hypocrites

First, let us make the definition of a hypocrite. A hypocrite is a person who pretends to be and live like a Muslim although he does not truly believe in Islam. A hypocrite sails under false colors and his intentions are at an odd variance with his actions.

We tend to divide hypocrites into two categories: creedal hypocrisy and practical hypocrisy. A creedal hypocrite is a person who pretends to be a Muslim while hiding his hostility against Islam and believers. This

---

[58] *Sahih al-Bukhari*, Adab, 69.

[59] Gülen, M. Fethullah, *Fasıldan Fasıla 2*, İstanbul: Nil, 2008, p. 291.

fact is expressed in the verse, *"Among people are some who say, 'We believe in Allah and in the Last Day,' although they are not believers"* (al-Baqarah 2:8).

A practical hypocrite is a person who has signs of hypocrisy in his actions and behaviors although he believes in Islam and its principles. In a *hadith*, our Prophet describes the basic characteristics of hypocrisy as follows: "There are three signs of a hypocrite: when he speaks he lies, when he promises he breaks his promise, and when he is entrusted he betrays the trust."[60]

As is clearly stressed in the *hadith*, lying is a sign of hypocrisy. And it is the first sign in the list. Unfortunately, Muslims do not attach due attention to this fact and they may easily resort to lies in their daily lives. For instance, a student who was late for the class may refrain from telling the real reasons for his being late and tell a lie instead. A friend calls us, but we don't want to talk to him. We may make someone answer the phone and say, "He is not here now," or "He is in a meeting." Although we know that we are completely wrong about a matter, we may come up with all sorts of lies to prove our case.

However, this is an extremely sensitive matter. A believer should be extremely alert against lies. "O people, what urges you to run after lies just as a moth jumps into fire?"[61] asks our Prophet, cautioning us be wary of all sorts of lies.

A Liar Betrays Himself

People may tell lies for different reasons. Research indicates the following as the main reasons for children to lie: bragging, pretending to be superior, attracting attention, acquiring affection, obtaining benefits, being ashamed, fearing to be ridiculed, being afraid of being punished, getting rid of painful or regrettable situations, fearing to lose status, and, above all, emulating adults and other children.

The following motives are listed for lying adults: obtaining benefits or warding off damages, taking revenge, humiliating enemies, showing

---

[60] *Sunan at-Tirmidhi*, Iman, 14.
[61] *Sunan at-Tirmidhi*, Birr, 26.

oneself as justified, earning other's respect with a sense of an inferiority complex, making it a habit to tell lies, and doing a favor to someone.

A person who tells a lie will eventually give himself up. A person may tell a lie with words, but not with his body. He cannot bring his whole body to subscribe to a lie. This is because human nature, created in the best disposition, does not permit this. For this reason, it is inevitable for a person who is not honest with he says to give himself up with some clues about the falsity of his words.

The changes that occur in the body while lying have been studied extensively. The findings of these studies can be summed up as follows:

1. The number of gestures decreases while people tell a lie. Normally, hand gestures are used to verify what we are saying. People use hand gestures unconsciously to emphasize their words. We may know that we are waving our hands while speaking, but we don't know what exactly our hands are doing.

If a person is telling a lie, he knows that his hands are doing something, but not exactly what, and this triggers a suspicion in him, urging him to decrease the movements of his hands. He may put his hands into his pockets or sit on them or hold one hand with the other, perhaps fearing that his hands may betray him. This self-contact may replace the act of holding the hands of the mother in times of distress, thereby alleviating the internal tension.

2. A person who lies tends to touch his face or edges of his face with his hands in increased numbers. During a normal conversation, people touch their faces with their hands only casually. The number of this gesture greatly increases during a conversion in which he is telling a lie. When we take our hands to our face during lying, we tend to hold our jaw, press on our lips, cover our mouth, touch on our nose, rub our cheeks, scratch the area below our eyes, pull our earlobe or toying with our hair. Among these, covering the mouth and touching on the nose are the more frequent movements.

Why does a person cover his mouth while lying? This is very obvious. People feel the need for seeking to catch the words or covering what they are doing. The mouth may be covered in various forms. Our fingers may move over our lips as if we are playing a trumpet; our index finger may be placed over our upper lip; or our hand may be placed next to our hand. Kids tend to close their mouth with their hands while lying. Of course, if a person takes hands to his mouth while talking, this does not necessarily means that he is telling a lie. If a person is hesitant about his remarks or afraid of making a mistaken or wants to buy time, he may take his hands to his mouth. For this reason, moving the hand to the nose is more refined and isolated movement compared to the act of covering the mouth. The hand that is moved to cover the mouth reaches the nose just above the mouth and in the end, a more symbolic and stylized movement is performed.

The most important reason for a person to take his hand to his nose when he is lying or is not sincere about what he says is physiological. Indeed, a person who experiences an internal tension due to lying may exhibit a number of physiological changes in his body. The blood pressure rises, and the heart rate increases and the sweat glands works harder and there is an itching sensation in the nose. It is not without reason that the nose of Pinocchio in Carlo Collodi's famous story would become longer while lying. Collodi discovered an important fact and used it in the children's literature with some exaggeration.

3. There is an increase in body movements of a person who is telling a lie. Uneasiness or discomfort of lying may urge people to change their position while sitting, by move forth and back in the seat. This positional change can be translated as "I wish I was somewhere else." These positional changes are more visible during panel discussions or conversations on TV. Even politicians who are seasoned liars are forced to make such movements in their seats when confronted with tough questions.

4. A liar tends to minimize his hand gestures while he waves his hands more frequently. By waving his hands gently, he may be trying to shake off the responsibility for what he says.

5. The facial expression on the face of a liar is generally very close to normal. Without specialization, one can hardly understand if a person is telling a lie or not simply by look at his facial expressions. One of the most important clues about a person's lying is that he tends to avoid eye contact.

The above-mentioned clues should not be taken as obvious and conclusive evidence about a person's lying, but as indicating the contradiction between our inner thoughts or feelings and our expressions. This contradiction may indicate a clear lie or insincerity, hesitation, or suspicion.[62]

READING TEXT
Ka'b ibn Malik: "My Truthfulness Saved Me"

Any discussion of truthfulness should always make mention of Ka'b ibn Malik. Ka'b was dexterous both in the use of swords and words. He was a poet. With his poems, he could demoralize the unbelievers. He had sworn allegiance to the Messenger of Allah at Aqaba. Therefore, he was among the first believers of Medina. But he couldn't attend the military expedition to Tabuk. Let us listen to him as he relates his own story:

"The call to join the battle was made to everyone because the fight would be fierce. However, this wasn't what Allah had ordained and the real fight didn't occur. The result of the battle might or might not have been revealed to the Messenger of Allah, but he was attaching special significance to the military campaign.

Like everyone else, I completed my preparations. Even, I had never prepared better for previous battles. The Allah's Messenger gave the signal and the army started to move. I didn't attend the army, thinking, 'I can catch up with them in any way.' I didn't have any particular job. But my self-confidence kept me behind. Delaying my departure to the next day, many days passed. I was no longer possible for me to catch up with the Messenger of Allah. I had nothing to do but wait for their return. But this waiting seemed ages to me.

Finally, the news of the return of the Prophet started to come. It was always the case. Medina would become alive soon before his return. The joy of the return of the Messenger of Allah was visible on everyone's face...

Finally, expectations were fulfilled, and the army arrived in Medina. As usual, our Prophet went to the mosque and performed two units

---

[62] Zuhal Baltaş and Acar Baltaş, *Bedenin Dili* (Body Language), pp. 143–144.

of Prayer and started to receive people. Everyone was coming to the mosque in groups and visiting him. Those who couldn't attend the campaign were expressing their apologies. Most of the people who were like me had cited excuses for not joining the campaign, and the Prophet had accepted their excuses. I could do the same as I had a special ability to persuade people and use the language and rhetoric. But how could I tell a lie to the Messenger of Allah although I had no excuse. I didn't do it; I couldn't. When we met, the Prophet greeted me with a wry smile that pierced through my heart. 'Where were you?' he asked. I explained my story as is. He turned his face away from me and said inaudibly, 'Go away.'

I went out. My people swarmed around me, saying, 'Tell an excuse and be free.' They were about to persuade me. But I came to my senses and asked, 'Are there others like me?' 'Yes,' they replied, and told the names of two people. Both were eminent Companions who had participated in the Battle of Badr: Murara ibn Rabi and Hilal ibn Umayya. They didn't cite any excuse, but told the truth. They were like me. I could follow their model. So I decided to do like them and avoid citing any excuse.

An order was issued about three of us, forbidding Muslims from speaking or meeting with us. The two others were staying at home, crying for their sins. I was younger and stronger. So I could walk in the streets and marketplace and I could go to the mosque at Prayer times. But none spoke to me. I was spending most of my time in the mosque. I would wait intently for a smile from the Messenger of Allah. To my dismay, I would return home in disappointment every day. Although there was always a smile on his face, the Messenger of Allah never looked at me nor smiled. I would greet him and wait intently for any answer from him. But his lips remained closed.

I would look at him out of the corner of my eyes while praying. He would look at me when I started to perform my Prayer. But he would turn his eyes away from me when I finished it. Fifty days passed in this state. All the people around me and the place I was living started to seem so alien to me that it felt like living in a foreign country.

One day, I jumped over the wall and entered the garden of Abu Qatada—he was my uncle's son and we loved each other very much—and
went to him. I offered my greeting to him. By Allah, he did not return
my greetings. I said: 'O Abu Qatada, I beseech you by Allah! Do you
know that I love Allah and His Messenger?' He kept quiet. I repeated
my question three times. Finally, he said, 'Allah and His Messenger
know better,' and left. The whole world seemed upside down. I never
expected to hear this from Abu Qatada. My eyes flowed with tears and
I sobbed.

One day, I was walking in the streets of Medina, and I heard a man
asking about me. The people began to point me out for him. He came to
me and handed me a letter. The letter was addressed to me. It was from
the king of Ghassan. The king invited me to his country. The following
was written: 'To proceed, I have been informed that your friend (the
Prophet) has treated you harshly. Anyhow, Allah does not make you live
in a place where you feel inferior and your right is lost. So, join us, and
we will console you.' When I read it, I said to myself, 'This is also a sort
of test,' and I took the letter to the oven and made a fire burning it.

When 40 out of the 50 nights elapsed, behold! There came to me
an envoy of the Messenger of Allah saying, 'The Messenger of Allah orders you to keep away from your wife.' I said, 'Should I divorce her; or
else what should I do?' He said, 'No, only keep aloof from her and do
not mingle with her.' I said to my wife, 'Go to your parents and remain
with them until Allah gives His verdict in this matter.' Meanwhile, the
wife of Hilal had asked permission to do Hilal's service. Hilal was a
helpless old man who has no servant to attend to him. The Messenger
of Allah gave permission to her. Some people suggested that I should
ask permission in the same way. But I didn't accept it. I didn't know
how the Messenger of Allah would react to me.

We remained in that state for 10 more nights, until the period of
50 nights was completed. My very soul seemed straitened to me and
even the earth seemed narrow to me for all its spaciousness. I had finished the Dawn (*Fajr*) Prayer on the fiftieth morning on the roof my
house, and I was sitting there. Then I heard someone calling my name.
'O Ka'b, be happy (by receiving good tidings),' he was saying. Real-

izing that relief has come with His forgiveness for us, I fell down in prostration before Allah. The Messenger of Allah had announced the acceptance of our repentance by Allah after the *Fajr* Prayer. I ran to the mosque. Everyone was congratulating me. Talha swiftly came to me, shook my hands and congratulated me. It was as if I was on the day of Aqaba. I went to the presence of the Messenger of Allah and held his hand. He, too, took my hand. The Messenger of Allah said, 'Allah forgave you.' Then, he recited the following verse:

> And (He turned in mercy also) to the three left behind and whose cases had been deferred (because they had not taken part in the campaign of Tabuk): (They felt such remorse that) the earth was too narrow for them despite all its vastness, and their souls became utterly constricted for them, and they came to perceive fully that there is no refuge from Allah except in Him. Then He turned to them in mercy, that they might repent and recover their former state (in Islam). Surely Allah is the One Who truly returns repentance with liberal forgiveness and additional reward, the All-Compassionate (especially towards His believing servants.) (At-Tawbah 9:118).

After this revelation, Ka'b ibn Malik told the Messenger, upon him be peace and blessings: "I promise to speak the truth as long as I live."[63]

QUESTIONS

1. "The opposite of loyalty is ...." Which of the following words best fills in the blanks?
   a. Integrity   b. Betrayal
   c. Truthfulness   d. Misguidance

2. Which of the following concepts is not directly related to "truthfulness"?
   a. Integrity
   b. Keeping agreements (keeping promises)
   c. Being straightforward
   d. Gratefulness

---

[63] Gülen, M. Fethullah, *The Messenger of God: Muhammad*, New Jersey: The Light, 2005, pp. 45–46.

3. Who was the Companion who said, "By Allah, this face is not that of an impostor" when he saw the Messenger of Allah?
   a. Abdullah ibn Amr
   b. Abdullah ibn Umar
   c. Abdullah ibn Mas'ud
   d. Abdullah ibn Salam

4. Who was the Companion who was converted to Islam saying that our Prophet had not told any lie during his life (the father of Ammar)?
   a. Zayd
   b. Yasir
   c. Abu Bakr
   d. Abu Quhafa

5. Our noble Prophet says, "Truthfulness leads to .... while lies to suspicion and hesitation." Which of the following words best fills in the blanks?
   a. Calmness
   b. Tension
   c. Success
   d. Power

6. Who is the Companion with the honorific title "Siddiq" (Loyal)?
   a. Abu Bakr
   b. Umar
   c. Uthman
   d. Ali

7. Certain behavioral changes are observed in a person who is telling a lie. Which of the following is not one of these changes?
   a. The number of gestures decreases while people tell a lie.
   b. A lying person takes his hand to his face more frequently
   c. A lying person makes more body movements
   d. A lying person looks directly into the eyes of his addressee

8. Who said, "Truth and dishonesty wrestle with each other until one removes the other from the heart"?
   a. Malik Deenar
   b. Ali
   c. Umar
   d. Hudhayfa ibn al-Yaman

9. Who is the Companion who said that his truthfulness saved him after he did not attend Tabuk campaign?
   a. Malik Deenar
   b. Sa'd ibn Ubada
   c. Ka'b ibn Malik
   d. Zayd ibn Haritha

10. "Lying is a sign of ...." Which of the following words best fills in the blanks?
    a. Virtue
    b. Knowledge
    c. Hypocrisy
    d. Power

6.

ETIQUETTE AND MANNERS

Good manners constitute a crown of Divine light
Wear that crown to get protection from all calamities...

What Does Etiquette Mean?

E tiquette can be defined as the set of good manners and behaviors, which are considered as part of the social custom, traditions, and rules book.[64]

It essentially refers to all rules about good manners, morality, good upbringing, courtesy, and politeness, and consists of the actions and behaviors that are considered nice by Islam. In this respect, etiquette consists of all good deeds, graces, and good conduct that people are expected to follow.

In other words, etiquette means acting in compliance with what Allah and His Messenger enjoin. For believers, the ideal etiquette rules consist of those which the Holy Qur'an teaches us and our Prophet, the Pride of Humankind, showed us with this exemplary life.

Social etiquette is essential for a community to safeguard its culture and civilization.

Allah the Almighty created man in the best stature both materially and spiritually.[65] He sent man to this world and endowed him with the blessings of this world. He sent down Divine Books and Prophets to

---

[64] *TDV İslam Ansiklopedisi*, 10:412, Istanbul, 1994.
[65] At-Tin 95:4.

guide people to the Straight Path and taught them with certain moral and ethical rules and principles.

In this context, our Prophet is our principal guide. Referring His Messenger, Allah commands, *"You are surely of a sublime character, and do act by a sublime pattern of conduct"* (al-Qalam 68:5). In a *hadith*, our Prophet asserts that he was sent to complement the fine morals.[66] A good many rules of etiquette can be found in his noble life as well as in his character.

The Messenger of Allah said, "Two qualities cannot coexist in a believer: parsimony and bad character."[67] He urged his Companions to adopt good conduct toward other people.[68]

The Prophet's orders and prohibitions regarding good conduct and etiquette concern everyone. For this reason, any person who has any duty for teaching other people good manners and conduct must apply these rules and principles to himself before moving on to engaging in other people's training.

Now, we will discuss the rules of etiquette a Muslim should pay attention to in the light of verses from the Holy Qur'an and the noble sayings of the Prophet.

1. *Hilm* (Gentleness)

Hilm means being inclined to gentleness or mildness; this adjective describes a person who is quiet and peaceful, slow to anger, quick to forgive, and who is in control of their lower nature. It also encompasses good morals because it embodies behavior like patience and tolerance in the face of unpleasant situations, keeping one's cool when provoked, and remaining dignified, serious and calm in response to distressing or unkind treatment. *Hilm*, along with humility, is one of the characteristics that most pleases Allah. In fact, these two dispositions are the source and origin of all other good character traits.

---

[66] *Al-Muwatta*, Husn al-Khuluq, 8; Ahmad ibn Hanbal, *Al-Musnad*, 2/381.
[67] *Sunan at-Tirmidhi*, Birr, 41 (1963).
[68] *Al-Muwatta*, Husn al-Khuluq, 1.

In addition to dignity and calm, *hilm* also means to act with conscious-ness and without haste. The result is a good and moral manner which pleases Allah. *Hilm* is one of the basic elements of good morality. With *hilm* it is also possible to perfect the mind and to improve other aspects of one's temperament. Just as knowledge can be gained through learn-ing, so *hilm* can be attained by making an effort. In other words, it is possible to reach *hilm* by working.

Hilm is also closely related to controlling one's negative responses and reactions. It is much more difficult for those who cannot control or reign their temper to attain a state of *hilm*. Scholars consider the ability to act with *hilm* to be among the most virtuous practices.

Humans are distinguished and privileged among all creatures. Allah the Almighty blessed people with lofty attributes that He endowed on no other creature, like intelligence, conscience, mercy, compassion, empa-thy, and the desire to help, respect, and honor. For this reason, the human being is the most valuable being in all creation.

As we can see, *hilm* indicates total gentleness, as well as behavior such as overlooking faults, forgiving others, and being open to everyone for the sake of dialogue.

READING TEXT
One Dream and Four Lessons

A Prophet had a dream one night.

In his dream, he was told: "In the morning, eat the first thing you come across and hide the second thing, and accept the third one, and don't hurt or sadden the fourth, and stay away from the fifth."

In the morning, the first thing he encountered a high-rise mountain and hesitated and couldn't know what to do. "How can it be possible? My Lord commanded me to eat it," he said to himself. But later he thought to himself, "Allah wouldn't command me to do something impossible," and started to walk toward the mountain with the inten-tion of eating it. But as he moved closer, the mountain became smaller and smaller and eventually turned into a sweet piece of cake, which he ate. Then he thanked and praised Allah.

He walked for a while and he came across to a golden bowl. "I was ordered to hide it," he said, and dug a hole and buried the bowl in it. He started to walk away from it, but he saw that the bowl came out of the hole onto the ground. Then, he turned back and buried it again. He had to go through the same sequence for three times, but in each case, the bowl came out of the hole. "I've fulfilled my Lord's order," he said to himself, and did not turn back.

He walked for a while before he met a bird. A hawk was trying to catch the bird. "O Messenger of Allah, save me," the bird pleaded. He accepted the bird's request and he hid the bird. But the hawk came to him and said: "O Messenger of Allah, I was hungry and I was trying to catch this bird since the morning. I was about to catch it. Do not leave me desperate of my sustenance."

Hearing the hawk, the Prophet did not know what to do. "I was ordered to accept the third thing I met, and so I did. I was ordered not to disappoint the fourth thing I met. Now that this hawk is the fourth thing I met, what shall I do now?" he asked to himself. He thought for a while and grabbed a knife and cut a piece of his flesh and threw it to the hawk. The hawk snatched it and flew away. Then, he took and bird out of its hiding place and released it.

He walked for a while and came across a carrion. In compliance with Allah's commandments, he walked quickly away from the carrion.

The night came. "O Lord, I did what you ordered me to do. Now please explain the meanings of these things to me," he prayed to Allah and fell asleep. In his dream, he was told:

"The first thing you met and ate is your anger. Initially, it is a like a mountain, but if you patiently suppress it, it will turn into a sweet cake.

"The second thing you met is good heed. Even if you try to hide it, it will come out eventually.

"The meaning of the third thing you met is this: you should not betray what is entrusted to you.

"The fourth thing means that when someone wants something from you, you should try to fulfill his wish, even by sacrificing something you really need.

"The fifth thing you met is backbiting. Keep away from those back-bite others."

A believer should be mild and should not give himself to outrage easily. He should try to perform good deeds.

2. Treating the Elderly with Respect

In Islam, the general rule is that those who are older than us should be respected, and those who are younger than us should be loved. In addition, it is commendable to care for those who have fallen on hard times. In fact, Allah's help reaches us through those people who need our help; our subsistence and sustenance may be increased for the sake of the adults and children whom we support.

The basic rule of respect for elders is even more important between family members. An example is the extra respect due to mothers and fathers. It is not proper to call our parents by their first names. Below are some of the *hadith* of the Prophet on this topic:

"If any young person shows respect to an older person because of the age difference, Allah will appoint someone to show him similar respect when he himself grows old."[69] This *hadith* informs us that young people will be rewarded for respecting elders and will be shown respect as they themselves grow old. Young people who perceive the elderly as a burden should think about this.

"The one who has no compassion for our little ones and does not honor our old ones is not one of us." This *hadith* summarizes the relationship between younger and older people in a clear and succinct manner. The blessed Prophet said, "To have respect for an older Muslim with graying hair shows one has respect for Allah."

In order to develop feelings of respect towards elders the following issues should be focused on:

> In all the family business of a household, the father and mother should be considered the authorities. This behavior encourages the internalization of respect for elders. A *hadith* says, "Blessings are to be found next to your elders."

---

[69] *Sunan at-Tirmidhi*, Birr, 15; *Sunan Abu Dawud*, Adab, 58.

The respect and reverence shown by parents to their own mother and father (i.e., the children's grandparents) serve as a great lesson to the children. If a child's mother and father are always compassionate, the child will be more aware of the duty and obligation to respect their parents and other elders. People develop this awareness over a long time and through habit. A child needs to see how to obey and respect elders over and over again to absorb this lesson. Otherwise it would be difficult—sometimes even impossible—to expect the desired result to come by simply teaching rules that are not practiced. Allah's Messenger expressed the critical need in a society for young people to maintain respectful attitudes and behavior toward those who are older than themselves: "If there were not white-haired elders, suckling babies, and grazing animals among you, calamities would have rained down on you like a flood."[70]

3. The Etiquette of Greeting

Greetings are a mark of fellowship enabling the strengthening of social bonds and increasing affection between human beings. It is also a Prophetic practice.

Offering a greeting is a recommended practice taken from the life of Allah's Messenger, while responding to such a greeting is religiously mandatory (*fard*). A *hadith* states: "You will not enter Paradise until you believe and you will not believe until you love one another. Shall I inform you of something the doing of which will enable you to love one another? Make the greeting common practice among you."

The etiquette of greeting can be enumerated as follows:

1. Saying *As-salamu alaykum* (Peace be upon you) when entering a gathering and before beginning to speak.
2. Saying *As-Salamu alayna wa ala ibadillahi's-salihin* (Peace be upon us and upon the righteous servants of Allah) when entering an unoccupied house.
3. Greetings can be extended when leaving an assembly or parting from one's companions as when meeting them, for Allah's Messenger says, "When one of you comes to an assembly, they should

---

[70] Ajluni, *Kashfu'l-Khafa*, 2/230.

offer the greeting (of peace) and when they intend to leave, they should leave with greetings (of peace)."

4. The initiator of greetings should be the younger person (when two people meet, or in general), the smaller party rather than the larger one, those riding over those on foot, and those who on foot rather than those who are seated.

5. If someone in an assembly responds with the words, *Wa alaykum as-salam* (And upon you be peace) when the assembly is greeted, others are relieved of the obligation to respond; however, if no one replies, everyone in the assembly is equally responsible.

6. The word *marhaba* has also been used in way of greeting. Allah's Messenger also used the term when welcoming his guests. Derived from the verb *rahaba*, it comes to mean, "Make yourself at home, you are among friends."

7. The response to the greeting should be given immediately and loud enough for the greeter to hear.

8. One should not pretend that they have not heard greeting of another.

4. The Etiquette of Sneezing

When a Muslim sneezes, they say, *Alhamdulillah* (All praise and gratitude are for Allah) If another Muslim is nearby, he or she says, *Yarhamukallah* (May Allah have mercy on you.) The recipient of this prayer then replies, *Yahdina wa yahdikumullah* (May Allah guide you and me to the right path).

Out of courtesy to those nearby, when one sneezes it is best to cover one's mouth, to try to limit the noise made, and to avoid spraying others by moving the head back and forth.

5. The Etiquette of Eating and Drinking

Allah the Almighty decrees that His servants consume the bounties He has conferred upon them, but that they not waste these. The following matters warrant utmost attention in regard to eating and drinking:

1. Hands must be washed before and after eating.

2. One must eat with their right hand, invoke the Name of Allah, reciting the *basmala*, at the beginning, eat from what is in front of them, and praise Allah at the end. Umar ibn Abi Salama narrates: I was yet a boy under the care of Allah's Messenger and I used to eat from all sides of the dish. So Allah's Messenger said to me, 'Dear child! Mention the Name of Allah, eat with your right hand, and eat from what is in front of you.' This is how I have eaten since."

3. If the *basmala* is forgotten at the start and remembered during the meal, one says, "In the Name of Allah at its start and end (*Bismillahi awwalahu wa akhirahu*)."

4. The meal must not been rushed, the food must be chewed thoroughly, the morsels must not be swallowed one after the other.

5. It is proper that one older in age or higher in position begin eating first.

6. Food must not be breathed upon in order to cool it. Actions and manner causing repulsion in others must be avoided. One must not speak or laugh when their mouth is full.

7. One must not look at what others are eating.

8. The person who prepared the meal must be thanked and acknowledged and one must help in setting and clearing the table.

READING TEXT
Accepting Invitations

The Qur'an says,

> O you who believe! Do not enter the Prophet's rooms (in his house) unless you are given leave, (and when invited) to a meal, without waiting for the proper time (when the meal is to be served). Rather, when you are invited, enter (his private rooms) at the proper time; and when you have had your meal, disperse. Do not linger for mere talk. That causes trouble for the Prophet, and he is shy of (asking) you (to leave). But Allah does not shy away from (teaching you) the truth.... (Al-Ahzab 33:53).

There are two basic elements that are important among the many aspects present in this verse. They are:

1. Waiting to be invited before joining a meal;
2. After enjoying a meal as a guest, not overstaying one's welcome or talking too much.

The revelation of this verse was occasioned by some people who would come to the Prophet's house unannounced at odd hours and stay, not wanting to leave until they had been served a meal. But clearly this is a general Islamic principle that is applicable to anyone who is a guest at someone else's home. Therefore, it is clear that one must not "invite oneself" or join a dinner or gathering without being invited. One day Abu Shuayb saw the Messenger of Allah among his Companions and understood from his face that he was hungry. He immediately said to his kitchen help, "Prepare a meal for five people, with me as the fifth. I want to invite Allah's Messenger tonight." Then he went over to the Prophet and extended the invitation. They walked back to his house together, but another man from the group followed them. When they reached Abu Shuayb's door, the Prophet said, "This man has followed me here. If you want, accept him; if you want, send him back." Abu Shuayb said, "No, O Allah's Messenger; he can join us too."[71]

In this *hadith*, if one looks closely, the Prophet was exercising Islamic *adab*. It is certain that believers take pleasure in hosting each other. But there are certain guidelines and boundaries that come with invitations and visits. An unannounced visitor can cause a host to worry, "What should I serve?" If they do not have much, this can in turn create financial hardship for them. At the same time, when a brother or sister in faith extends an invitation to a fellow Muslim for a meal or a visit, it should be accepted, as this will foster affection and closeness between them. This is stated in the *hadith*, "When you are invited, accept the invitation."[72] Nafi also said, "Ibn Umar accepted invitations to weddings and other invitations, even when he was fasting." When one is invited, it is not good manners to reject or to avoid acceptance. The following *hadith* shows that not accepting

---

71 *Sahih al-Bukhari*, At'ima, 57, 34; Buyu, 21; Mazalim, 14; *Sahih Muslim*, Ashriba, 138, 2036; *Sunan at-Tirmidhi*, Nikah, 12, 1099.

72 *Sahih al-Bukhari*, Nikah, 71, 74; *Sahih Muslim*, Nikah, 103, 1429; *Sunan at-Tirmidhi*, Nikah, 11, 1098; *Sunan Abu Dawud*, At'ima, 1, 3736–39.

invitations and showing up somewhere without being invited are both examples of poor manners: "He who does not accept an invitation which he receives has disobeyed Allah and His Messenger. And he who enters without invitation enters as a thief and goes out as a plunderer."[73]

6. Cleanliness and the Etiquette of Bathroom

The first requirement for deserving Allah's love, entering His Presence, and being His servant is cleanliness. It is the first thing we must do to put ourselves in the correct state for performing obligatory Daily Prayers, which are the "ascension of the believer." In the following verse Allah decrees performing ablution or taking a bath for this purpose: "*O you who believe! When you rise up for the Prayer, (if you have no ablution) wash your faces and your hands up to (and including) the elbows, and lightly rub your heads (with water) and (wash) your feet up to (and including) the ankles. And if you are in the state of major ritual impurity (requiring total ablution), purify yourselves (by taking a bath)*" (al-Maeda 5:6).

With this verse the ablutions before the Ritual Prayers became obligatory and all Muslims wash their hands, faces, mouths, noses, ears, necks, and feet before each of the five Daily Prayers.

Just as we should keep our body and the clothes we wear clean, we also need to keep our living quarters and the places where we worship clean. The Qur'an says, "*O children of Adam! Dress cleanly and beautifully for every act of worship*" (al-A'raf 7:31).

Allah's Messenger made it an obligatory practice to bathe at least once a week (this was at a time when frequent bathing was uncommon). He also instructed people to "keep your environment clean" and urged them to maintain the shared community spaces as well. A *hadith* recounts his words on this subject: "Avoid two cursed things," he said, and when the Companions asked "What two things?" he replied, "Relieving oneself on the road where people pass by, or in a shady place (where people take a rest)."[74]

---

[73] Ibid.
[74] *Sahih Muslim*, Taharah, 68; *Sunan Abu Dawud*, Taharah, 15; Ahmad ibn Hanbal, *Al-Musnad*, 2/372.

The noble Messenger, who was "the Living Qur'an" and who embodied Qur'anic morality, as with everything, was the best of examples in cleanliness. He was very careful about his own cleanliness and whenever he lay down or got up, day or night, he washed his mouth and nose, brushed his teeth and made ablutions. In particular he emphasized that cleaning the teeth is crucial not only for the health of our mouth, but also to please Allah; moreover, he taught that the first thing a person should do on waking from sleep is to wash their hands. He was also careful to dry his limbs on a towel after washing.[75]

Allah's Messenger paid close attention to cleanliness throughout his life; he would wear clean, nice clothes whenever he out went in public, particularly to the mosque or to visit someone. He used pleasant scents and avoided eating onions, garlic or smelly foods before going out.

The following issues concerning bathroom etiquette must be especially observed:

1. Prior to entering the bathroom, men must first roll up their trouser legs and remove their socks.

2. One is advised to say, *Allahumma inni a'udhu bika minal khubthi wal khaba'ith* (O Allah! Verily, I seek refuge in You from the filthy and impure) before entry.

3. One must enter with their left foot first and exit with the right foot first.

4. Men must not urinate in a standing position, but while sitting. (Urinating while standing damages the kidneys, adversely affects the soundness of the Prayer, and this constitutes the cause for the greater part of punishment in the grave.)

5. One must not speak, consume anything, idle around or think of matters pertaining to the Hereafter while in the bathroom.

6. Cleaning must be performed with the left hand. (The vessel containing the water, as well as the tap and the door must be held with the right hand and any items for cleaning such as brushes with the left hand.)

---

[75] *Sunan at-Tirmidhi*, Taharah, 40, (53).

7. The bathroom must be left neat and clean. (Washing the hands and leaving the toilet clean.)

8. Males must ensure that *istibra* is performed after urinating (waiting for a certain period to ensure that no urine has remained in the urethra).

7. Meeting Etiquette

We attend various meetings in our lives. In order to make our meetings conform to the very spirit of verses and *hadith*s, we should pay attention to the following principles:

1. We should take note of the date and place of the meeting beforehand and go to the meeting in a timely manner.

2. The place of meeting should be properly arranged by the host. (Adjustments should be made to the lighting, cleanliness, sound, and temperature system for efficient work.)

3. If the start of the meeting is delayed, this spare time should be properly utilized (reading, resting, etc.)

4. We should be well-prepared before going to the meeting (fulfilling our responsibilities, getting the materials we may need such paper, pen, etc.)

5. During the meeting, we should explain our case in the best way possible and we should not insist on our case if it does not receive broader acceptance.

6. We should be dressed in an appropriate manner without causing any distraction. We should always be friendly and should not talk unnecessarily.

7. We should be respectful toward older people as well as people who are more informed than us.

8. We should not leave the meeting unless we really need to do so. We should ask for permission before leaving. (We should not let other business sneak into the meeting.)

9. We should not whisper or speak in secret to another person when we are with other people.

10. We should leave our cell phones outside or shut them off or turn their volume down.

11. Refreshments should be prepared moderately and served properly.

12. We should ask permission if we cannot attend the meeting because of an important reason.

13. Our attire should be tidy and clean and we should be properly shaved.

14. We should speak our mind when we are consulted. We should refrain from speaking needlessly to contribute to clamor.

15. We should refrain from disclosing people's faults to the public and we should not embarrass them.

16. We should speak our mind about the decision taken at the meeting, asking for clarification. We should not criticize those decisions after the meeting is over.

> *Knowledge should mean a full grasp of knowledge:*
> *Knowledge means to know yourself, heart and soul.*
> *If you have failed to understand yourself,*
> *Then all of your reading has missed its call.*

8. Etiquette for Talking or Giving Advice to People

People communicate with each other by talking. Kind words open the doors of hearts. In the Holy Qur'an, Allah the Almighty commands us to use the best style in our communications, saying, *"And say to My servants that they should always speak (even when disputing with others) that which is the best"* (al-Isra 17:23).

The duty of a Muslim is to be able to communicate his message to his addressee in a clear manner and without hurting anyone. The following noble saying of our Prophet should be our guiding light: "The evil tongue fouls any gathering."[76]

Now, let us list the points we should take into consideration in this context:

1. We should follow our word by greeting our addressees. We should ask how they are doing.

---

[76] *Sunan at-Tirmidhi*, Birr, 47.

2. We should use proper titles with our addresses.

3. We should use formal language with our elders. We should not be on a first-name basis with them.

4. We should use a warm, respectful, and affectionate language and tone. We should avoid hurting anyone.

5. We should respond to the people who call on us in a respectful manner.

6. The volume or manner of our talking should not lead to discomfort of our addressee (too high or too low voice, etc.)

7. We should refrain from overstatements or understatements about any person (in his presence).

8. We should not speak unnecessarily.

9. We should stay away from backbiting or gossip. We should not use crass or obscene language.

10. When a question is asked, we should give a short and clear answer if we know the answer. We should not respond with assumptions if we don't know the answer.

11. We should give others a say. If we want other people to listen to us, we should first learn to listen to them.

12. For a speech to be effective, the orator should have firm faith in it and act sincerely and be able to make his audience feel his sincerity. We cannot be convincing with our speech if we don't believe in it.

9. The Etiquette of Entertaining Guests

One of the major aspects that contributes to strengthening the ties of brotherhood, getting to know one another and sharing/solving problems, is visiting socially. This is why the Islamic faith gives particular importance to Muslims visiting one another. In one of the traditions, the noble Prophet gave the tidings that a person who visits the sick or another Muslim has prepared his place in Paradise.

A believer should pay frequent visits to those he loves, in particular his parents and family and never abandon them, not only during times of happiness but also during times of calamity and affliction. In the Islamic faith, this is known as maintaining the bonds of kinship. Maintaining the bonds of kinship means to visit family and friends, to inquire after their health and wellbeing. Unfortunately, like many of our other values, we neglect keeping in touch with our family and friends. The younger generations of today are brought up deprived of the love and affection of their grandparents, uncles and aunts. Maintaining the bonds of kinship, which the noble Prophet said would be the means of entering Paradise, is not simply visiting relatives but also means taking care and protecting them in every way possible.

The mentioning of kinship after obligatory worships such as Prayer, the fast and giving charity reveals the importance of the topic in the Islamic faith. Here is just one example from the Qur'an:

> Keep from disobedience to Him in Whose name you make demands of one another, and (duly observe) the rights of the wombs (i.e., of kinship). ... Allah is ever watchful over you. (An-Nisa 4:1).

There are various degrees of maintaining the bonds of kinship.

1. We must be polite and speak with kindness towards our most distant relatives, bestow our greetings when we see them, inquire to their health and wellbeing, and always have a good opinion and want good for them.

2. We should pay regular visits to closer family members and always assist them whenever necessary. This is more in terms of physical assistance. In particular, visiting the elderly members of the family occasionally and helping them will make them extremely happy.

3. Maintaining the bonds of kinship with the closest and most important family members means giving financial help and support. It is our duty to comply with the general rules of visiting, and in addition visiting these family members especially on Eid celebrations, and never severing the ties of kinship.

POINTS THE HOMEOWNER SHOULD OBSERVE

1. The homeowner should personally welcome and bid farewell to his visitors.

2. He must welcome his visitors with a smile, clean-shaven and with clean clothing.

3. He should receive his guests in decent clothing (not shorts, pajamas, vest, etc.)

4. The rooms or sections of the house to be used by the guests should be clean and tidy.

5. The other habitants of the house should also welcome the guests and display their happiness to see the guests.

6. The guests should never be left alone or become bored.

7. The host should make a special effort in serving guests. Whatever is given should be placed on a small table or somewhere suitable, and an atmosphere of happiness and pleasure should be created.

8. A host must pay attention to his guests, should ask if they need anything, and meet their requirements.

9. A host should never scold or criticize others in front of his guests.

10. If the guest is wearing a jacket or coat, the host should take it and hang it up.

11. The host should give his guest slippers on entering the house.

12. Guests should be entertained in a tidy room in which they will feel comfortable.

13. If the visitors are the guests of our elders, then we should only remain in the room when required and take into consideration that they may want to speak privately.

14. If there is no objection to us being present, then we should not speak more with the guests than the host, as interfering in the conversation unnecessarily is not suitable.

15. Even if this visit coincides with the most difficult, most troublesome period, we should never show this to our guests so they do not assume that we are disturbed at their presence.

16. If we sit our guests in a room, we should pay attention to the following: If we are unable to remain in the room with the guest for any reason, then another member of the household should entertain and sit with them. It would be rude to leave the guest alone in the room.

17. If the guest has come from a distance, then we should prepare dinner without even asking, and we should sit with the guest at the table.

18. While we are sitting with the guests, we should not check the time frequently so he does not assume we want him to leave.

19. We should never speak and laugh secretly in front of a guest.

20. It is not right for others to peep around the door of the room where the guest is sitting without saying anything. Either the door should not be opened at all, or if the door is opened one should inquire as to the health and wellbeing of the guest. If we have time limitations for any reason, we should at least apologize, ask permission and then leave the room.

21. When the guest is leaving, we should hold their jackets or coats and express our emotions of pleasure and gratitude at their visit.

22. We should wait at the door until the guest leaves and not close the door immediately.

23. If the guest is going to stay overnight, the place he is to sleep should be prepared, the bedcovers and sheets must be clean, and we should provide towels and pajamas if necessary.

THE RULES A GUEST SHOULD OBSERVE

1. When the door of the house is opened, the guest should not stand where he can see inside.

2. A visitor should knock on the door three times and not persist in knocking if no one opens the door. The noble Prophet said, "Knock on the door three times; if you are not granted permission to enter, then you should leave." This can also be considered the same in terms of using the telephone.

3. When a guest enters and leaves he should bestow his greetings. A person should bestow greetings even when he enters an empty house.

4. A guest should never arrive late for an invitation but should arrive early.

5. When a person visits, he should wear clean, tidy clothing.

6. If possible, a visitor should not go to someone's house empty-handed but should take a gift.

7. A guest should knock on the door and enter only after permission is given by the host.

8. A guest should avoid looking around and inspecting the room and causing the host any inconvenience. A guest should not offer anything to another guest without the permission of the host. He should sit in the place allocated by the host and ask for permission to go to the bathroom.

9. The guest should not find fault with any food that is given, and even if there is a problem with the food, he should not make this apparent.

10. A visitor should not ask for the food or drink he wants, but rather should be satisfied with what is given and never ask for a specific food saying, "Do you have this?" If the homeowner asks what a guest wants to eat by specifying certain foods, the guest should chose the easiest, most convenient to prepare.

11. We should take certain points into consideration—such as the host's age, his family or illness when visiting—and pay attention to our manner of speech. In particular the elderly and unwell expect us to visit often; however, these visits should be short. Therefore, we should pay more frequent visits to these individuals than we do to others.

12. Even if religious beliefs or political opinions are different from those of the host, the guest must not say anything to upset the host or those present.

13. The guest should leave expressing his gratitude and pleasure.

14. A guest should not leave without the permission of the host.

15. If the host is busy, the guest must shorten his stay and ask permission to leave.

16. When a person is unable to visit for any reason, he should inform the host beforehand and asked to be excused.

READING TEXT
Visiting Neighbors and Other Friends

The following *hadith* speaks of the necessity of visiting neighbors and other friends. According to a narration by Qays ibn Sa'd, one of the Companions, Allah's Messenger came to visit him one day, stayed in his house for some time, prayed for him and then left his home. Another tradition recounts that the Prophet visited a family of the Ansar, ate a meal in their home, performed his *salah* (Prayer), and prayed for them while he was there. Abdullah ibn Qays also witnessed that "The Messenger would visit the Ansar, both individually and as a group. When he visited them individually, he went to their homes; when he wanted to see them as a group, he would go to the mosque."

In light of the above narrations, it is clear that the Prophet visited Muslims often, and he always asked how they were doing. We can also see that the Prophet's Companions continued the practice of visiting each other, even when they lived in different regions. They would cross great distances to visit one another for the sake of Allah, even though traveling at that time incurred great difficulties. Salman, for instance, went from Midian to Damascus to see Abu al-Darda.

Abdullah ibn Mas'ud had the following conversation with his friends who came from Kufa to Medina to visit him: Abdullah asked, "Do you sit together and share your problems?" and his friends answered, "We have never neglected doing so." Abdullah then asked, "Do you visit one another?" The friends replied, "Yes, O Abu Abdurrahman; in fact, if we have not seen some of our Muslim brothers for a long time, we walk all the way to the other end of Kufa to see them and to ask how they are." Abdullah replied, "As long as you continue to do this, you will live in peace."[77]

10. The Etiquette of Public Speaking

Here follows a list of principles that need to be considered when speaking kindly and giving effective advice:

---

[77] Kandahlawi, quoted from the translation of *Hayat as-Sahaba*, (The Prophet's Companions' Way of Life), Vol. III, 1115.

1. It is helpful if the addressee or audience can easily follow the line of thought in your talk, and pick out the main ideas. Any kind of address can be made more effective by using clear transitions to signal the end of one point and the beginning of the next, and therefore listeners will know when the topic is changing. The main ideas should be pointed out at the beginning so that the audience can see where the speech or conversation is heading and how it is related to them.

2. If the audience cannot determine how the conversation or advice is applicable to them, the natural result is that they will lose interest in the subject. Therefore, when introducing a topic, one should state at the beginning how the advice can benefit those listening.

3. Ending a talk by saying something like "That is all I have to say" is unsatisfactory and reduces the effectiveness of the conversation or speech. The end of any speech is in fact more important than the introduction. To finish a talk in a compelling way one should reemphasize the purpose or main point of the speech, and the speaker should aim to inspire the listeners; after this the speaker should close by expressing pleasure for attention shown and thanking the listeners.

4. Advice should be clearly given and explained well; evidence should be provided for anything that others are to understand or accept.

5. Do not be afraid to speak the truth.

6. When addressing people, speaking about anything that is not useful knowledge concerned with religious or communal principles should be avoided. It should be obvious and clear to the audience, from the moment one begins to talk, what the subject is and what kind of things are going to be said about it.

7. Not even the smallest word, allusion or gesture that implies a form of ridicule or scorn should be included in any advice.

8. No matter what the topic of the advice or exhortation, the speaker will ultimately reveal something of their own personality. They should keep in mind that it is unfeasibly difficult to incite others to laudable actions without offering their sincere opinion on the issue. For advice to be effective, it is crucial that the speaker truly

believes what they are saying; the audience should be able to perceive this belief. It is useless to try to make others believe what one does not believe oneself.

9. Keeping a serious tone and composure while speaking to an audience or giving advice is preferable.

11. The Etiquette of Science and Scholarly Studies

A believer hunts for opportunities to boost his knowledge. Indeed, as our Prophet put it, it is an obligatory duty for every Muslim to learn something new.[78] Islam attaches great importance to learning and boosting our knowledge. Indeed, its first commandment is "read." The following noble sayings of our Prophet about learning are quite striking: "Wisdom is the lost property of the believer; wherever he finds it he has the right to take it."[79]

In the Holy Qur'an, our Lord commands: *"Say: 'Are they ever equal, those who know and those who do not know?' Only people of discernment will reflect (on the distinction between knowledge and ignorance, and obedience to Allah and disobedience,) and be mindful"* (az-Zumar 39:9). In this verse, Allah keeps the people of learning apart from other people and holds them in high esteem.

In line with the very spirit of this verse, our Prophet indicated that there are two enviable people: the one whom Allah endows with wealth and makes him succeed in spending that wealth in Allah's cause and the other whom He endows with wisdom (knowledge) and makes him teach that wisdom to others.[80]

Yes, every believer should be eager to learn something new and read books to boost his knowledge. At the same time, he should implement in his daily life what he learns from books and share his wisdom with others.

In doing so, we need to take into consideration certain rules and principles of etiquette of learning:

---

[78] *Sunan ibn Majah*, Muqaddima, 17.
[79] *Sunan at-Tirmidhi*, Ilm, 19.
[80] *Sahih al-Bukhari*, Ilm, 15.

1. We should not think we are learning something new just because our parents want us to do so.
2. We should not let failure intimidate us.
3. We should be well-prepared and eager to attend courses.
4. We should pay full attention to the teacher.
5. We should ask our teachers to re-explain the topics we fail to understand.
6. We should seek advice from successful students about how they become successful.
7. We should follow a regular schedule.
8. We should choose a suitable place for study.
9. We should do our best to learn our topics.
10. We should not move on to other topics before understanding the current one.
11. If there are applicable parts of the topics we learn, we should apply them.
12. We should sever our ties with the people who may make us hate learning.
13. We should be respectful and humble toward our teachers.

There are also certain principles which teachers should consider: These can be listed as follows:

1. They should try to be equipped with the most advanced knowledge in their branches; they should closely keep track of innovations; and they should not attend courses without preparation.
2. They should be able to simplify the topics according to the level of students and they should not discourage students by presenting matters the hard way.
3. They should act as model for students with their morality, life, behavior, and words and they should inspire respect in their students. They should not forget that they cannot attain respect just by asking for it. Teachers who frequently reprimand students and want them to show respect and exert pressures on them to force them to show respect are the least popular teachers.

4. Teachers should love their profession and try to teach what they know to their students in the best way.

5. Teachers should be affectionate toward their students and they should refrain from spoiling the hard-working students while scorning the lazy ones.

6. They should not embarrass their students by publicly talking about their faults, and they should be tolerant and forgiving.

7. They should deal with the problems of their students and listen to them and be concerned about their pains and sorrows. However, they should not act unceremoniously with their students while doing this, and they should maintain the honor of their profession.

8. They should not use grades to punish students and they should be fair in giving grades to the students.

9. They should safeguard their dignity and honor by staying away from expensive gifts or feasts from students or their families.[81]

READING TEXT
Studying and Learning

Someone who lives an exemplary life and tries to please Allah by teaching other people and sharing knowledge is on the Path of Allah, and Allah is indeed pleased by such a person. Kathir ibn Qays explains, "I was in the Mosque at Damascus sitting beside Abu al-Darda. A man came and said, 'O Abu al-Darda, I came from the Prophet's city of Medina to ask about a *hadith* that I have heard you are relating.' Abu al-Darda, in order to find out whether this was really the man's intention, asked, 'Could you also have come to do business (trade)?' 'No,' he answered, 'I did not come to do any such thing.' He asked again, 'So you did not come for anything else other than to hear a *hadith*?' The man replied, 'No, I came only because I heard that you know *hadith*.' Only when he had established that the man had truly come to win Allah's pleasure did Abu al-Darda say, 'I heard the Prophet of Allah say, "Allah will make the path to Paradise easy to anyone who takes to

---

[81] Halit, Abdülkadir, *Adab-ı Muaşeret* (Social Etiquette), İstanbul: Rehber, 2005, pp. 126–127.

the road looking for knowledge. Angels lower their wings over the seeker of knowledge, being pleased with what he does. All the creatures in the earth and sky, even the fish in the sea, pray for Allah's help and forgiveness for those who acquire knowledge. The superiority of the scholar over the worshipper is like the superiority of the moon over the stars (i.e., in brightness). Scholars are the heirs to the Prophets. For the Prophets left neither dinar nor dirham (units of money) but knowledge as their inheritance. Therefore he who acquires knowledge has in fact acquired an abundant portion."

The following points can be deduced from the *hadith*:

1. Any effort or endeavor that is expended on acquiring knowledge is counted as effort or struggle made on Allah's way, and this leads a person to Paradise. To put it simply, the path of knowledge is the path to Heaven; what a beautiful path it is. The angels come to the aid of one who is on this path, and all creation offers prayers for them.

2. The difference between the scholar and the follower is like the difference between the moon and stars, for knowledge is a light that illuminates a person's whole surroundings and the community of the knowledgeable person. It shows the right path to everyone. However, a person who simply follows, even if they perform a great deal of supererogatory worship, does not benefit others in the same way. Their worship benefits only themselves. Those who choose knowledge, on the other hand, bring blessings down upon themselves and all those around them.

3. Scholars are the heirs to the Prophets; the only thing the Prophets left as an inheritance was knowledge. When scholars choose the path of learning and the pursuit of knowledge, they win the honor of inheriting the legacy of the Prophets. One of the Prophet's Companions, Abu Hurayra, was almost always at the Prophet's side. He would listen to all the Prophet's teachings, carefully memorizing his sayings. One day in Medina, he spoke aloud to the people milling about on the street: "The Prophet's inheritance is being divided up; why are you wasting time here? Go and claim your share!" The people said, "Where is it being dis-

tributed?" Abu Hurayra said, "In the mosque." So they ran to the mosque. But soon they turned around and came back, and Abu Hurayra asked, "What's happened?" They said, "We went to the mosque, but we did not see anything like what you said being distributed." So he asked, "Was there no one in the mosque?" They answered, "Yes, we saw some people; some of them were performing *Salah*, some were reading the Qur'an, and some were talking about the permissible and the prohibited." Hearing this, Abu Hurayra told them, "Shame on you. That was the Prophet's inheritance."[82]

QUESTIONS

1. Which category of rules is not included in the social etiquette?
   a. Morality   b. Upbringing
   c. Courtesy   d. Punishments
2. Which of the following is not a source of the social etiquette?
   a. Our Prophet's Sunnah   b. Human custom
   c. Traditions   d. Laws and regulations
3. What are the two qualities which don't coexist in a believer?
   a. Generosity and bad character
   b. Parsimony and bad character
   c. Asceticism and backbiting
   d. Hostility and mildness
4. Which of the following best fits to the description, "being inclined to mildness"?
   a. Fidelity   b. Courtesy
   c. Gentleness   d. Bashfulness
5. Which of the phrases best fills the blank in the *hadith*, "The one who has no compassion for our little ones and does not honor our old ones ...."?
   a. Is not one of us.
   b. Should be prepared for his place in Hell.

82 Halit, Abdülkadir, *Adab-ı Muaşeret* (Social Etiquette), İstanbul: Rehber, 2005, p. 120.

    c. Is cursed.

    d. Is damned.

6. Which of the following does our Prophet mention as the factor for boosting love among people in his *hadith* in which he said entering Paradise requires having faith and having faith entails loving each other?

    a. Being mild-mannered

    b. Showing compassion to the elderly

    c. Greeting everyone

    d. Being courteous and polite

7. Which of the following statements about greeting is incorrect?

    a. The little ones should greet the older ones first.

    b. The group with fewer members should greet the group with more members first.

    c. Those who are sitting should greet those who are walking first.

    d. Youths should greet the elderly first.

8. Which etiquette is the phrase "Yarhamukallah" (May Allah have mercy upon you) related to?

    a. The etiquette of dining   b. The etiquette of greeting

    c. The etiquette of conversation   d. The etiquette of sneezing

9. Which one of the following does not comply with the etiquette of dining?

    a. To cool down the meal by blowing upon it

    b. Eating the food that is closer to us

    c. Eating the food using our right hand

    d. Reciting the Basmala before eating

10. Which of the following phrase best fills in the blanks in the sentence, "………….. are the heirs to the Prophets"?

    a. Officers   b. The elderly

    c. Scholars   d. Young people

APPENDIX

The Importance of Reading

The purpose of learning is to make knowledge a guide for your life, to illuminate the road to human perfection. Any knowledge that does not fulfill these functions is a burden for the learner, and any science that does not direct one toward sublime goals is only deception.

Reading means learning. Reading means knowledge. It is to improve comprehension. It is not an activity that starts and ends at specific times in life. It is a lifetime activity. It is the only power that defeats ignorance and false beliefs. "Reading is the noblest passion." It helps people to know themselves better. It guides them in their relations with other people. Those people who don't read books don't know how to behave in most cases.

Reading teaches people why they live. It makes them cry at times and make them laugh at others. But in any case, it reminds people that they are human beings. Reading opens up our inner worlds. Reading expands the limits of people's small worlds, helping them to meet with blessed people and learn how they become blessed, and show them the ways for becoming like the blessed people.

Read is like going on a long and enjoyable journey. First, you set a range and then a route. Then, you set off. With every step or progress, the passenger's enthusiasm increases. He increasingly forgets about the road and route. He just walks on, perhaps without noticing that he is walking. He sees and observes many beautiful places and things. He adds these to his knowledge and enthusiasm and moves on.

He travels the whole world over the book pages. Sometimes, he travels to the Age of Happiness to breathe in the very atmosphere of our Prophet, peace and blessings be upon him, and meets His Companions. Sometimes, he may travel back in time or he may be absorbed in deep thought about the future. Eventually, he boosts his knowledge, and he resumes his journey by collecting dreams, chasing after thoughts and augmenting his power of intuition. For great thinker Cemil Meriç, book is a "door to the unknown" and reading is the "key that unlocks the door to the unknown inside us."[83]

Numerous people of great stature who illuminated the epochs of our glorious past used this key to enrich their knowledge and wisdom and led fruitful lives. Therefore, we, too, must stick to reading. Reading should be a passion for us.

1. The Holy Qur'an Attaches Great Importance to Reading

We have studied the words related to reading in the Holy Qur'an. We found that there are 87 "qiraah" (reading) and derivatives, 336 words meaning "writing," 780 "ilm" (knowledge) and derivatives, 117 "hikmah" (wisdom) and derivatives, 18 "tafakkur" (reflection) and derivatives, and 49 "aql" (intellect) and derivatives.

Isn't it very interesting? Obviously, our Lord attaches great importance to reading.

We all know that the first order of the Holy Qur'an is to "read." But there is also another chapter (Al-Qalam) in which Allah swears on the "pen" (*qalam*) and on "what they write with it line by line," which further testifies to the significance of knowledge and learning in Islam. Indeed, by swearing on something, Allah glorifies it and brings it to our attention.

Now, let us read some of the selected verses concerning the importance of reading:

---

[83] Cemil Meriç, *Bu* Ülke (This Country), pp. 111–113.

1. *"He grants the Wisdom to whomever He wills, and whoever is grant-ed the Wisdom has indeed been granted much good. Yet none except people of discernment reflect and are mindful"* (al-Baqarah 2:269).

2. *"Say: 'Are they ever equal, those who know and those who do not know?'"* (az-Zumar 39:9).

3. *"Of all His servants, only those possessed of true knowledge stand in awe of Allah"* (Fatir 35:28).

4. *"Above every owner of knowledge, there is (always) one more knowl-edgeable (until Allah, Who is the All-Knowing)"* (Yusuf 12:76).

2. The Noble Prophet Prescribes That We Read

When we study books on the traditions of the noble Prophet (books of *hadith*), we see that in many of the traditions he praised knowledge, schol-ars and students of knowledge, encouraging his followers to read and learn. The noble Prophet, who said that acquiring knowledge was incum-bent upon all Muslims, also said in another of the traditions that wisdom and knowledge are things the believer lacks, and that a believer should acquire knowledge wherever he finds it. He emphasized that the ink of scholars will be weighed on the Day of Judgment along with the blood of martyrs, and the ink of scholars will outweigh the blood of martyrs.[84]

The noble Prophet related in another tradition, "He who follows a path in quest of knowledge, Allah will make the path to Paradise easy for him. The angels lower their wings over the seeker of knowl-edge, being pleased with what he does. The inhabitants of the heav-ens and the earth and even the fish in the depth of the oceans seek forgiveness for him. The superiority of the learned man over the devout worshipper is like that of the full moon to the rest of the stars. The learned are the heirs of the Prophets who bequeath neither dinar nor dirham but only that of knowledge; and he who acquires it has in fact acquired an abundant portion."[85] And he also supplicated occasionally with these words: "O Lord! Benefit me with what You

---

[84] Ibn Abdilbar, *Jamiu Bayani'l-Ilm*, 33.

[85] Ibn Abdilbar, *Jamiu Bayani'l-Ilm*, 37; *Sunan at-Tirmidhi*, Ilm, 19; *Sunan ibn Majah*, Muqaddima, 17.

have taught me, and teach me what is beneficial for me, and increase me in knowledge."[86] The noble Prophet, who distinctly prescribed that we read and increase our knowledge said, "Allah raises nations with knowledge, making them leaders of goodness whose guidance and paths are to be followed."[87] Another narration reads, "The learned believer holds a rank seventy degrees higher than a devout servant. The distance between each of these degrees is like the distance between the heavens and the earth."[88]

In the same way that the Prophet encouraged studying and attaining knowledge, he also tells us to convey this knowledge to others. "The greatest charity for a Muslim is to learn something and then teach it to his Muslims brothers."[89] And in another tradition: "Allah, His angels, the dwellers of the heavens and the earth, even the ant and the fish in the ocean supplicate for those who teach people knowledge."[90]

READING TEXT
How Do the Companions Explain the Importance of Reading and Learning?

Our Companions had certainly made numerous precious remarks about learning and reading. We cannot quote all of them here. So we made a selection for you.

Muadh ibn Jabal: The Unlucky People Are Deprived of Knowledge

Being one of the Companions who were tasked with the duty of teaching people, Muadh ibn Jabal explains the importance of knowledge as follows:

"Study knowledge, for learning it for the sake of Allah is truly fearing Him. Seeking it is worship, revising it is glorification of Allah, searching for it is a type of jihad, teaching it to those who do not know it is

---

86 *Sunan at-Tirmidhi*, Da'awat, 128.
87 Ibn Abdilbar, *Jamiu Bayani'l-Ilm*, 66.
88 Haythami, *Majmau'z-Zawaid*, 1/132.
89 *Sunan at-Tirmidhi*, Ilm, 7; *Sunan Abu Dawud*, Ilm, 10.
90 *Sunan at-Tirmidhi*, Ilm, 19.

a charity, and giving it to those who deserve it; is a means of drawing near to Allah. Knowledge is the discerning proof of what is right and what is wrong, and it is the positive force that will help you surmount the trials of comfort, as well as those of hardships. Knowledge is a comforting friend in times of loneliness. It is the best companion to a traveler. It is the innermost friend who speaks to you in your privacy. Knowledge is your most effective sword against your foe, and finally, it is your most dignifying raiment in the company of your close comrades. Through knowledge, Allah, blessed be His Name, raises some people in rank, and He makes them leaders in righteousness and models in morality. The vestige of their faith is avidly sought, their deeds are emulated perceptively, and people will seek and sanction their opinions solicitously and unequivocally. The heavenly angels seek their company and anoint them with their wings, every fresh or withered life they pass by implore Allah the Almighty to forgive them their sins, even the fish in the oceans, the beasts of the lands and every bird of prey and migratory bird pray and solicit the mercy of Allah the Almighty on their behalf. This is because knowledge revives the dead hearts and drives them out of darkness into light, and because knowledge is the light of the inner eyes that cures one's blindness and restores his inner sight. By acquiring knowledge, an ordinary slave can attain the degrees of the eminent people as well as high stations in this world and the next. Reflection is like fasting and deliberation is equal to the Night Prayer. With knowledge, one can be aware of the rights of relatives as well as what is permissible and forbidden in the religion. Knowledge is the leader of deeds and deeds follow knowledge. Good people are lucky to have knowledge while those who are deprived of knowledge are unlucky."[91]

Knowledge Increases with Deeds

Kumayl ibn Ziyad narrates what Ali ibn Abi Talib, may Allah be pleased with him, told him about knowledge: "Ali ibn Abi Talib held my hand once, and he walked with me out of the city to the open desert. When we got to the desert, he took a deep breath before he said to me:

---

[91] Abu Nu'aym, *Al-Hilyah*, 1:239, Dar al-Kitab al-Arabi, Beirut, 1405; Ibn Abd al-Barr, *Jami Bayan al-Ilm*, 1:55.

"'O Kumayl ibn Ziyad, hearts are like vessels, and the best are exceptionally conscious and vast. Learn from what I am going to tell you! There are three types of people: (i) a godly scholar (*alim rabbani*), (ii) a student who is seeking salvation (*muta'allim*), and (iii) a ferocious follower of every howler and his own type (*hamaj ra'a*). The third type of people is biased, and they float with the currents. They neither seek enlightenment through knowledge, nor do they take refuge in a safe recess during a storm.

"You must understand that knowledge is better than money, for knowledge will guard you, while you have to be the guard of your money. Deeds are more exalted than knowledge, while money needs someone to spend it justly in order to render it pure. To love a man of knowledge and to learn at his hand is a debt one can never repay. Knowledge earns its owner respect during his lifetime and praiseworthy remembrance after his death, while what money can do expires once it is spent. The keeper of a safe dies and what he guards and the treasures remain, however, a man of knowledge lives throughout the ages.

(And he pointed to his chest) Here, indeed here.

"There is knowledge if only I could find bearers for it. But instead I have found them quick to comprehend but not trustworthy—they use what pertains to the Religion for worldly ends, they seek to use Allah's proofs against His Book, blindly following the people of truth but having no Insight regarding receiving it. Doubt pierces his heart when anything problematic arises. He is neither this nor that! Or one passionately addicted to pleasures, accustomed to following desires. Or one given to amassing wealth and piling it up. And these are not from the callers to the Religion. They are most like the grazing cattle. And thus knowledge passes away with the passing away of those who carry it. Oh Allah yes, the earth will not be without one who stands upright for Allah, with proof so that Allah's proofs and clear signs are not abolished. They are the ones who are few in number but having most value to Allah, with them Allah asserts His proofs amongst their contemporaries and cultivate them in the hearts of ones similar to them. With them knowledge assaults and comes upon the true state of affairs so that which those accustomed to easy living find difficult therein, they find easy and they are at home with that which causes consternation to the ignorant ones. They live in this world with their bodies whereas their souls are attached to higher things. They are Allah's ambassadors in His land and the callers to His Religion! Oh how I would like to see them and I seek Allah's forgiveness for myself and for you. If you wish then stand."[92]

Abdullah ibn Umar: Knowledge Is of Three Types

"Knowledge is of three types:

1. Allah's Book that is forever speaking (the Qur'an).

2. The Prophet's established Sunnah.

3. Saying, 'I do not know.'"

He once said: "Knowledge consists of the Allah's Book (the Qur'an) and the Prophet's Sunnah. If you say something as your own opinion outside these, I don't if you find it among your good deeds or bad deeds."[93]

3. We Can Discover the Secret of the Universe Only by Reading

Our Lord has two books with which He makes Himself known to us and which He requires us to read. These are: the book of the universe and the Holy Books revealed to the Prophets, particularly including the Holy Qur'an. The book of the universe is already pointing us to our Lord, but with his vast mercy on his servants, Allah also sent down real books so that they don't falter and go astray in the Straight Path. By expounding His words in these books, He confirms what the book of the university is telling.

It is our duty to read both of these books to understand the purpose of creation and lead a life in compliance with the Divine Will. Every man should ask himself: "What am I? Why do I exist? Where do I go from here?" and try to discover the secrets of the universe.

---

[92] Abu Nu'aym, *Al-Hilyah*, 1:79, Dar al-Kitab al-Arabi, Beirut, 1405.

[93] Ibn Abd al-Barr, *Jami Bayan al-Ilm*, 2:26.

Reading is of course will be our greatest assistant in this quest. Indeed, thanks to reading, man can understand himself, the reason for his existence, his Creator and the secrets of the universe. The Holy Qur'an is already calling us to "read," isn't it? Whoever complies with this injunction will be able to discover the secrets of existence, start to adopt a different perspective with the universe and lead a more conscious life.

4. We Must Get Rid of Disgrace of Ignorance

As poet Mehmet Akif Ersoy put it, ignorance is the archenemy of individuals and nations. In one of his poems, he refers to ignorance as the real enemy:

> *O real enemy, we must kill you at once*
> *You are the one who keep our enemies above us.*

As you know, the period before our Prophet became the Messenger of Allah is called the Age of Ignorance (*Jahilliyya*) while the period after he became the Messenger is referred to as the Age of Happiness. Have you ever thought about the reason? This is because ignorance makes the ignorant person and his circles unhappy. As a matter of fact, being a Muslim means getting rid of ignorance and unhappiness associated with it. Indeed, a Muslim reads and keeps away from ignorance and what will make them unhappy. Thus, he attains peace both in this world and the next.

The archenemy of humanity is ignorance as it is the source of all evils in the world. It is a disgrace both for individuals and societies. For this reason, we cannot get rid of this disgrace until we complete our learning both in religious and material sciences.

Fethullah Gülen draws attention to this fact as follows:

"The Holy Qur'an whose first order was "read" wants us to study the universe and man as if we are reading a book and learn about Prophet Muhammad, peace and blessings be upon him, who is our guide in reading these books. This is the very purpose of the creation of man. Man is supposed to look, see, think, load new things to his brain every day and travel into diverse climates; this is the goal set for him. This goal entails a marriage of religious and physical sciences.

For this reason, every believer should study both religious and positive sciences and be equipped with science, knowledge, and wisdom. Therefore, we should read books and ponder what we read while we are home, at work, at the restaurant, at the bus station, in the car and on the road, and we should waste even the shortest moment of our time. Indeed, an empty person has nothing to give others. If we are not sufficiently knowledgeable at least about the philosophy, logic, fundamentals and encyclopedic summaries of physics, chemistry, astronomy, medicine, botany and the like, and if we are not informed about religious science at least the same level, then we will not able to tell anything to other people or persuade them, but also we will be doomed to be carried away by the winds of misguidance. So, we, as the entire nation, should come to our senses and kick off a campaign for getting rid of the disgrace called ignorance.[94]

The historical truth is that the nations who chose to remain ignorant by failing to read were continuously exploited. This applies to our time as well. Today, the nations who cannot possess, control, or benefit from information or use it instrumentally will continue to be colonies of the information societies.

Indeed, ignorant nations do not have any benchmark or criterion in their minds or at their hands and therefore, they are prone to all sorts of ideas indoctrinated on them. All sorts of false beliefs, superstitions, enmities, discord, dissension and material and spiritual problems are rampant in such societies. For this reason, we must read to move from the darkness of ignorance to the light of knowledge.

5. Reading Is the Best Way to Learn

"Books are silent teachers," says a famous thinker. In fact, every book is a teacher as like a teacher, it informs us and teaches how to learn. Scholars and scientists categorically assert that reading is the easiest and

---

[94] Fethullah Gülen, İnancın *Gölgesinde* (In the Shadow of Faith), 2:203–204, Nil Yayınları, İzmir, 2002.

most effective way for man to learn. Indeed, they acquire most of their knowledge by reading.

Students who are successful in central exams note that reading books has a major place in their lives. Experts note that reading books contributes great to success at exams.

Yes, reading is the easiest way to learn. Authors write down books that are result of years of work and study. By reading those books, one can learn that experience in just one day. Is there any business that is more profitable than this?

Of course not. Indeed, knowledge is a basic need for all of us so that we can learn how to live and put our ideals into practice and take confident steps into future. Reading and learning should be our path if we want to keep up with contemporary, civilized, and prosperous nations.

6. Reading Brings Renewal

In the flow of life, anyone, may wither and live without enthusiasm from time to time. But remaining alive is one of the duties of the believer. It is unavoidable for one without a fresh influx to become brittle and lifeless, like a tree without water. No matter what stage of life one is in, one must produce something, and one's action is directly proportional to one's reading. To be up and running, to have forward momentum and action, depends on reading.

A believer reads to retain his liveliness. The readings will be constant and regular. For those who share the same goals, coming together and discussing books will increase the benefits. Those people who renew themselves and strengthen their faith within the written word will be firmer in their resistance against withering.

Perhaps it is possible to escape the suffocating atmosphere of over-familiarity by reading something less customary, such as the sacred lives of those Companions who wrote their names in golden letters on the pages of history. Perusing the golden tableaus of their lives, while escaping from the enticing, poisonous beauty of this transient world, and pouring the truth of what we read into those who thirst, we will restore our balance through reading.

7. Reading Is What We Need to Attain
Companions' Awareness

The Companions of our Prophet would not spend an idle moment in their lives, but read and study books to attain the goal Mr. Gülen referred to above. Indeed, the following advice Abdullah ibn Mas'ud, an eminent Companion, gave to his students sums up our Companions' perspective on knowledge: "Be the sources of knowledge and learn and lanterns of guidance. Illuminate the darkness of the night with your self-study at home. Let your hearts be fresh and your cloth old. Let yourselves be known to those in heaven and hide your identities to those on Earth."[95]

Clearly, our Companions are very eager to read and learn, thereby maintaining their vitality. You must have heard about Ashab al-Suffa. This is a community of Companions whose sole purpose to acquire knowledge and attain Allah's pleasure by doing so. They would spend most of their time by reading books and studying and guiding people about how they should implement Islam in their daily lives.

Angels would envy them and send them breezes of Divine relief with their wings. Uqba ibn Amir, a member of this community, narrates: "One day, the Messenger of Allah asked, "Which one of you wants to go to Bathan (a place near Mecca) in the early morning and own two beautiful camels?" "We all want this, O Messenger of Allah," they replied.

Who would not want it? Camels meant everything to them. At that time, a camel roughly corresponded to a luxury car today. And the Prince of Prophets was talking about having two camels.

Our Prophet continued: "It is better for you to learn two, three, or four verses from the Qur'an early in the morning than to have two, three or four camels, respectively."

Hearing this advice, one should rush to learn more, shouldn't we? Our Prophet said, "My Companions are like stars, whomever among them you follow, you will be guided." And if we want to follow the way of the Companions, we should read and learn.

---

[95] Ibn Abd al-Barr, *Jami Bayan al-Ilm*, 1:126.

READING TEXT
What Were the Last Words of Muadh ibn Jabal?

At night, Muadh ibn Jabal asked, "Has the morning come?" The Companions next to him did as they were told and returned. "Not yet," they said. After a while, he asked once again, "Go look. Has the morning come?" They went outside to see if it was morning. "Not yet," they replied once again. After a while, he asked the same question, but this time, they said, "Yes, the morning has come." Then, Muadh ibn Jabal said:

"I seek refuge in Allah from the night whose morning leads one to fire. Hello, death! Hello! You the visitor who pops up after vanishing from the sight! You the friend who comes to the rescue! My Allah, I was afraid of you, but now I want you. My Allah, You know well that I don't want to stay in this world in order to build canals and plant trees. I just wanted to live so that I may attend the scholars' circles of teaching and learning even at the expense of withstanding the hardships of the world or suffer from thirst of the world."[96]

8. Books as Faithful Friends

In saying, "I lived with books and found peace with them. I loved the person in the book more than the person out on the street," the late Cemil Meriç aptly expresses what a faithful friend books are.

Indeed, books are loyal companions that are with us at each and every moment. From time to time, we complain of not being able to find our friends by our side in times of difficulty, whereas books are not thus. They are right beside us whenever we need them. Even if we are disloyal and do not turn their pages them for a long period of time, they patiently wait upon dusty shelves, take no offense, and do not respond with the same unfaithfulness. They embrace us with their knowledge and gnosis. They satiate our spirit and soothe us, and mold our lives.

And in doing so, they do not expect gratitude. They are always giving, as they are our congenial companions. That is why we had better not neglect them. Let us not leave our old friends upon dusty shelves, in attics or packed up in boxes. Look at what Muslim scholar Al-Jahiz, who

---

[96] Abu Nu'aym, *Al-Hilyah*, 1:239, Ibn Abd al-Barr, *Jami Bayan al-Ilm*, 1:51.

leased libraries and read until morning, has to say in praise of books: "I know no animal product that despite its youth, the short time that elapsed since its birth, its modest price and its ready availability brings together so much excellent advice, so much rare knowledge, so many works by great minds and keen brains, so many lofty thoughts and sound doctrines, so much wise experience or so much information about bygone ages, distant lands, everyday sayings and demolished empires, as a book. It is a visitor whose visits may be rare, or frequent, or so continual that it follows you like your shadow and becomes a part of you.

Silent when silence is called for, it is eloquent when asked to speak. It is a bedside companion that does not interrupt when you are busy but welcomes you when you have a mind to it, and does not demand forced politeness or compel you to avoid its company... A book is a companion that does not flatter you, a friend that does not irritate you, a crony that does not weary you, a petitioner that does not wax importunate, a protégé that does not find you slow, and a friend that does not seek to exploit you by flattery, artfully wheedle you, cheat you with hypocrisy or deceive you with lies."

9. Books Constitute a Measure of Civilization

Books constitute a measure of civilization. Civilized societies have made progress thanks to books. The nations that placed knowledge, wisdom, and research at the very center of their lives have always been a major player in the international arena. Our glorious past is rife with incidents that exemplify this truth:

In the Middle Ages, the Muslim world had huge libraries containing more than tens of millions of books. In the 10th century, the Muslim world was ahead of Europe for 200–300 years both in both terms of librarianship methods and size of compilations. In medieval European libraries, books would be chained to the bookshelves and when someone wanted to read a book, the book would be chained to a lectern. Another weird measure was that people would be allowed to read books only behind gratings.[97]

---

[97] Summarized from Necip Asım Yazıksız, *Kitap 10* (Book 10), İletişim Yayınları, Istanbul, 1993.

In the 10th century, Andalusia was way ahead of Europe in terms of knowledge and wisdom. For instance, the personal library of Al-Hakam II housed some 600,000 manuscripts. 400 years later, King of France Charles V, known as "the Wise," had only 900 books in the royal library.

There are multiple examples of this.

Ottoman Sultan Yavuz Sultan Selim, whose brief reign saw numerous conquests, took three mule-loads of books with him when he launched a military campaign against Egypt. As a prince, he would sleep only three hours a day and dedicate eight hours of his day to reading books.

When he died at the age of 63, eminent Islamic scholar Fakhruddin ar-Razi had left behind 200 works. If we put his books one top of each other, they will exceed our height. His Qur'anic commentary is alone 12,000 pages. He must have written 15–20 pages daily, including during his childhood, to finish this work. Most of the time, he would continue to read books even while eating.

Imam Abu Hanifa, the founder of the Hanafi school of Islamic jurisprudence, had answered 500,000 questions studying the Holy Qur'an and the Prophet's Sunnah, and he had issued 4,000 *fatwas* (edicts).[98] This could be possible only by reading and evaluating what he read.

Rumi (Mawlana Jalaluddin) would read and study books and acquire knowledge night and day. His wisdom continues to illuminate the minds and hearts of millions of people for centuries.

Famous *mufassir* (Islamic scholar specialized in the Qur'anic commentaries) Sayyid Qutb would dedicate 10 hours to reading books every day. "I have spent 40 years of my life by reading," he would say.

These examples are thought-provoking lessons showing us the very foundations our civilization and culture and providing us with guidance about what we should do in return. Our ancestors in whose deeds we take pride in gave books, reading and learning a major room in their lives.

Now it is our turn. We should make plenty of reading and work for the promotion of our beloved country and we should market our civilization as a model for attaining bliss both in this world and the next. Other-

---

[98] Mustafa Kara, *Tekkeler ve Zaviyeler* (Dervish Lodges), 15, Dergah Yayınları, Istanbul, 1990.

wise, we will make no headway, but be dragged from disaster to another. This fact is stressed by our famed thinker Cemil Meriç as follows:

"A nation that turns itself into a mass will not be everlasting. A mass of people who are primarily concerned with money cannot survive. We despise intellectual activities. Shouldn't we be ashamed when we compare the money we spend on books with what spent on horse races? We make fun of people who are fond of books, but we are happy with racegoers. No one has ever become miserable because of books. However, there are numerous people who went bankrupt due to horse races. The best book can be bought at the price of a turbot. But who's buying? If public libraries were as costly as official banquets, they would be honored more by our government. If books were worth one-tenth of bracelets, ladies and gentlemen may be tempted to read them once in a while. Many people don't buy books because they are cheap. They don't understand that the sole value of a book is found in its being read, and studied in depth several times."[99]

READING TEXT
The Importance the Ottoman State
Attached to Books

The Ottoman Empire held books in high esteem as sultans, their wives, viziers, and pashas would finance the construction of organizations of science and learning. They also established wealthy foundations to ensure their continued funding. Upon conquering Istanbul, Sultan Mehmed the Conqueror overhauled the scientific institutions and libraries. The first libraries of Islam include the Hagia Sophia, Zeyrek, and Eyüp Sultan libraries as well as the libraries located within the Fatih Mosque complex. Sultan Mehmed donated 2,000 books to the Eyüp Sultan Mosque and 3,000 books to the Fatih Mosque. Other Ottoman sultans, too, continued to see books and libraries as precious as they established new libraries or enriching the existing ones. These works and cultural assets were destroyed for many times throughout history.

---

[99] Cemil Meriç, *Bu* Ülke (This Country), 109–110, İletişim Yayınları, Istanbul, 1992.

All of imperial mosques contain madrasas, schools, and libraries within their complexes. Many statesmen and benevolent people obtained the sultan's permission to establish madrasas and libraries.

Let us give an example about the place of books and knowledge in the Ottoman Empire: "Sultan Murad IV started the military campaign against Revan (Yerevan) in 1634 and returned from it in 1935 and with a heartfelt sincerity, he changed his course: for 10 years, his life was full of military campaigns and actions and he had seen many wars and incidents. He had also performed his pilgrimage. In line with the *hadith*, 'We have returned from the lesser jihad to greater jihad,' he would try to focus on acquiring knowledge and learning the religious science. He had decided to dedicate his sustenance and salaries to the ways of learning.

As he was returning to Istanbul, he had examined the books in the bookstores of Aleppo. With a Divine inspiration, the Sultan wrote down the names of the books and upon returning to Istanbul, he spent money to buy these books and delved into an intense study. In 1637, he managed to study these books. For 10 years, he read and studied books day and night. He had the opportunity to study the majority of sciences. When he was indulged in the enthusiasm for reviewing a book, he would study in the candle light until the sunrise and he wouldn't feel exhausted or frustrated."[100]

In the Ottoman Empire, the people who engaged in calligraphy would be held in high esteem as a sign of the importance attached to artists and scholars. Many Ottoman dignitaries would invite a calligrapher to their mansions and asked them to write down pieces from the Holy Qur'an, *Sahih al-Bukhari* (the most popular and most reliable *Hadith* collection) or *As-Shifa* (the famous book in which Qadi Iyad described the miracles of our beloved Prophet, peace and blessings be upon him). Many rich Ottomans would regard the income obtained through calligraphy as a perfectly permissible income and they would earn money by writing down books using this art although they didn't need the money. But they would allocate this money to pay for funeral and burial costs when they die.[101]

---

[100] Necip Asım Yazıksız, *Kitap 105 ve 107–108* (Book 105 and 107–108), İletişim Yayınları, Istanbul, 1993.

[101] Necip Asım Yazıksız, *Kitap 56–94* (Book 56–94), İletişim Yayınları, Istanbul, 1993.

10. A Person Reaches Perfection by Reading

A person reaches perfection by reading because reading is the sustenance of the soul, the source of development. When a person reads he realizes his lack of knowledge, and while studying a person's desire to learn increases. Basically, every book that is read whispers the need for reading and stimulates even more reading. Therefore, reading and studying become a way of life to the extent that a person must read on a daily basis.

Our past is vibrant, so to speak, with people devoted to studying. Here are a few examples:

When the great scholar Hammad ar-Rawiyah was asked if he would ever be satisfied with the knowledge he had attained he replied, "I used all my resources but never reached the limits of knowledge. As I passed over one mountain another appeared before me."

The Abbasid caliph Al-Ma'mun had an elderly uncle who had grown tired of attaining knowledge and asked, in shame, "Is it befitting for us to study at this age?" The caliph answered, "It is better for you to die acquiring knowledge than to live being content with ignorance."

On his death bed Abu Yusuf, one of Imam Azam's students, lost consciousness; then he opened his eyes and began to discuss a topic of knowledge with a man at his bedside. One of those present said, "While you are in this state, try to rest." Abu Yusuf replied, "If only my fate would come to me while I was occupied with learning and depart from this world attaining knowledge."

Qatada ibn Di'amah, one of the great scholars and successors of the Companions, strived throughout his entire life to attain knowledge. One of his students, Matar al-Warraq, conveyed this in these words: "Qatada continued to learn until the time of his death."

Astronomer Pierre Simon Laplace: On his death bed at the age of seventy-eight, his last words were: "What we know is little, and what we are ignorant of, is immense."

Samuel Johnson, who died at the age of seventy-five and wrote the first English dictionary, began to learn the Dutch language just a few years prior to his death.

Indeed, a person should strive to utilize and benefit from every moment and regret time wasted on things of no avail to the soul, mind and heart. As for those who do not put the time they possess to good use, for them there is no present; they always focus on the future. To those who say, *Let's wait and see, it is still early, we will fulfil our duties in the future*, the best reply is surely, *If now is not the right time, when is?* The phrase "Tomorrow begins today" summarizes this nicely.

11. Reading Books Enlightens Our Homes

Books are like lambs for our homes. A person who read books at home illuminates both his house and his heart. Parents should read books and make sure that their children see them read books. They should even specify a book reading time at home during which all members of the family should read books. To this end, a special book reading place may be set.

Looking at the history of Islam, we can see that houses are the places where the Qur'anic verses are recited.

Many Companions were first converted to Islam at the house of Al-Arqam ibn Abi al-Arqam. When he was sent to Medina for teaching Islam to Medinans, Mus'ab ibn Umayr stayed as a guest at the house of As'ad ibn Zurara. The house of Makhrama ibn Nawfal was a Dar al-Qurra (a house dedicated to the teaching of the Holy Qur'an).

When they came to Medina shortly after the Battle of Badr, Abdullah ibn Umm Maqtum and Mus'ab ibn Umayr became guests of this house. It is historically known that in one of these houses, Khabbab ibn al-Arat taught the Holy Qur'an to Zayd ibn Amr and Fatima bint al-Khattab.

In his never-ending fight against ignorance, Bediüzzaman Said Nursi advises in his books that we should turn our homes into schools where all members of the family regularly read books.

Therefore, we should read books at home and organize learning-oriented programs at home and we should work do our best to read books. Every parent who seeks to raise his children in the best way should try to make this happen. Encouraging children to read will be our best legacy for them.

12. Reading Brings Us Closer to Our Lord

A curious and sincere reader increases his knowledge, understands his own poverty and weakness, sees that he is in fact nothing, and realizes that all the power and strength lies with Allah. Such reading brings the person closer to Him. The Qur'anic verse, *"Are they ever equal, those who know and those who do not know?"* (az-Zumar 39:9) points out the superiority of readers.

Let us see how our noble Prophet explains the way reading brings humans closer to Allah: "At home the candle tears through the darkness and shows things, by alighting beneficial knowledge, illuminating the heart, raising the curtains, moving the person away from *masiwa* (everything other than Allah), it brings him closer to Allah, may His glory be exalted."

The Messenger of Allah, peace and blessings be upon him, said "Scholars are the inheritors of the Prophets" (*Sunan at-Tirmidhi*). Indeed, the righteous and devoted scholars, who in terms of knowledge and morals are the inheritors of the Prophets, are certainly the means of guidance and prosperity.

Reading works that will make one closer to Allah the Almighty is praiseworthy. Even more commendable is to take one's reading beyond theory by seeking ways to bring one's knowledge into practice, for one's servanthood depends on daily improving one's performance. The essence of *ilm* (knowledge) is practice, and its purpose is to come closer to the All-Compassionate.

Our noble Prophet stated, "He who is asked about knowledge (of religion) and conceals it, will be bridled with a bridle of fire on the Day of Resurrection."[102]

Human being is like a perfect ever-renewing machine, and a marvelous and ever-changing palace. He need constant renewal through reading, contemplation, prayer, and good deeds. In Sufi terms, to become *al-insan al-kamil*, the perfect soul or the universal human being, is the real meaning and purpose of existence. Perfection can be attained through reading,

---

[102] *Sunan Abu Dawud*, Ilm, 9; *Sunan at-Tirmidhi*, Ilm, 3.

but reading alone does not suffice. The knowledge obtained through reading must be supported by righteous deeds.

13. Reading Keeps the Brain Young and Active

Henry Ford, founder of the Ford Motor Company, claimed, "Anyone who stops learning is old, whether at twenty or eighty. Anyone who keeps learning stays young. The greatest thing in life is to keep your mind young."

According to the latest studies, approximately fifty thousand neurons die every day in the brains of people over twenty years old. An increase in the death of these cells causes memory loss. Memory loss begins to set in rapidly with the increasing death of these nerve cells in those who do not read, whereas a person who reads regularly has a greater chance of avoiding this condition, because reading helps preserve the brain cells. If we want our brains to remain young and healthy we must constantly stimulate them. Reading challenging material frequently is good brain exercise. In recent years, the fatal disease known as Alzheimer's has increased rapidly throughout the entire world. This disease, which is the diminishing of the brains' abilities, affects many people over the age of sixty-five. In fact, according to research, Alzheimer's disease is one of the leading causes of death.

Research shows that one of the causes of this disease spreading among elderly people is the lack of brain exercise. Brain cells that are not exercised or used properly begin to diminish. As cultural involvement decreases, nerve cells in the memory center of the brain begin to degenerate and die. Reading exercises the human brain and keeps the brain alive and healthy. This is why dementia or memory loss in old age is less common in people who read on a frequent basis compared to those who are not accustomed to reading.

This true story is relevant to this subject: In America, when Supreme Court Justice Oliver Wendell Holmes retired voluntarily at the age of ninety, he was visited at his home by newly elected President Franklin D. Roosevelt. The President asked why Holmes was reading Plato in his library. Holmes replied, "To improve my mind." Students who suffer from memory loss should concentrate more on reading books and not accustom the brain to idleness.

14. Reading Opens up Our Horizons

The people who regularly read books will soon realize that their horizons are broadened. Reading helps people to adopt a more objective, more encompassing and broader perspective to the matters. Thus, their approach will be more accurate.

A journalist asked a person who was an educator and a philosopher the following question on his 90th birthday:

"What is the use of so many books you've read, sir?"

"It helps me to climb the mountains," replied the educator, implying that this process of reading has improved his knowledge and culture. The journalist didn't understand this fine point, and asked again: "Climb the mountains? What is it good for?" The philosopher replied,

"You need to climb the mountains in order to see other summits you can climb."

Reading helps us to keep away from short-sightedness, bigotry, and shallow-mindedness. A person who likes to read books is at peace with himself and his environment. In a society with such people, problems and disputes are easily resolved in a civilized manner. Ignorant people who don't like to read books try to settle their problems with quarrels, brawls, bullying, and violence. Any solution attained in this way never works over the long haul.

READING TEXT
Books Enrich Us

We can say that we are at a crossroads, given the failure of the education system in which all of us stay for a certain period. Books are invisible educational tools. If we don't use these tools, we may have to suffer from the failed education system all through our lives. It is really important for us to stand next to books, travel through their pages, meet the truth and grow up in the refractions of their light. Our readings are building us; we are the sum of what we read. Books enrich us; they give us refreshing drops.

The act of reading improves and renews our symbols, helping us to make sense of changes around us and most importantly, facilitating the way we know ourselves better. When we open a book's cover, there are "us" and "fragments from us" in the book. We collect these fragments from books and collect them constantly. With every book we read, we take a step forward and grow up and become bigger.[103]

15. Why a Student Should Read

Just as reading enables students to acquire metal prowess, it also develops thought function. It is well known that reading is conducive to richness of thought and actively engages the brain. Children who read also facilitate the work of parents and educators in the education process. Parents sending their children to expensive schools to see their educational investment pay off and enabling their children to attain everything they want is not sufficient, as children without a habit of reading have difficulty becoming good learners.

The cognitive function of generations who do not read is gradually atrophying, their capacity to generate ideas regressing, and they are unable to form sound communication with their environment due to their inadequate vocabularies. The inculcation of universal values, character and personal development, and a historical and cultural consciousness are only possible through the raising of generations who read, research and who possess a love of learning. During the education process, children need to improve themselves through reading. Regrettably, our children who are growing up watching television and playing computer games are increasingly losing their capacity for reading and are being deprived of the opportunity and possibility that reading provides. The thoughts of children who read and are read to are richer when compared with their peers. Due to the fact that thought develops in parallel to knowledge, a child can only think to the extent of what they

---

[103] Nihat Dağlı, *Sızıntı*, September 1997, Issue: 224. Also see Nihat Dağlı, İnsanı Kitaba Çağırmak (Calling on People to Books), Kaynak Yayınları, İzmir, 1996.

know. Thoughts unsupported by information remain shallow. Reading increases the child's vocabulary and contributes positively to communication skills. Children who have acquired a habit or reading exhibit an increased communicative capacity. It ought to be stressed that individuals who are able to express themselves well in today's information and communication society are those who are successful. Regular reading facilitates children's learning and develops their ability to make accurate judgments. The mental capacity that books provide contributes to a person's personal maturation through their positive impact on learning, inquiry and decision-making processes.

"The brain functions actively during reading, and a great many dynamic functions, cognitive information processing and memory-making processes are used actively. During reading and thinking, there is a recognized increase in the glucose burnt in many different parts of the brain. As a result of reading, different intelligence functions such as concentration, attention, comprehension and interpretation, as well as perceiving what is observed, develop in a positive way.

READING TEXT
To Acquire a Historical Awareness

Our lives are under constant change like any living organism, and our lifestyle, actions, behaviors, and attitudes have their share from these changes. Change is the invariable characteristic of life. Yet there are certain values we need to stick to for maintaining our culture and civilization. In this context, historical awareness is what helps us to survive as a society and stand on a firm basis in the face of the ongoing changes in the world.

The societies with historical awareness will not only ensure that their national consciousness does not disintegrate, but also avoid morbid moods. The societies that lack this awareness cannot be themselves, but will come under the influence of others, changing their colors and turning them into tools and toys for other societies. This in turn leads to fragmentation. The people who don't learn lessons from the history of their own nation and who cannot benefit from that history will seek true happiness in other nations. They will imitate not their technologies or development, but their behaviors and attitudes that should not be emulated, which eventually results in a great corruption.

Indeed, history is not a simple parade of the incidents that don't concern us; it is also the life itself as presented to us. It is the historical awareness that saves us from being rootless and turns us into a river flowing into eternity and helps us to feel our presence among the nations that share the same fate."[104]

Knowledge of history is a major factor in the formation of our national awareness. It heavily relies on historical awareness; the historical awareness that is deprived of it is destined to dry up like a flower that is without water.

Our nation needs a generation of people with historical awareness more than ever. Indeed, historical awareness is a perfect guide for getting back to the right track. It is at the same time a safeguard for the nation.

Today, we cannot attain this awareness if we read only about the past wars. Books that do not tell lies, but describe the real history should be prepared to this end. We desperately need history books that examines the past events with respect to their real causes and effects instead of giving a phlegmatic account of them, the books that contain analysis of past incidents taking into consideration the conditions of the time and their significance for our own time.

READING TEXT
A Lesson from the Past

In the past, there was valiant wrestler who had defended his title as the chief wrestler of the traditional Kırkpınar wrestling tournament for 26 years. His name was Kel Aliço (Aliço the Bald). No wrestler could challenge him. In the 27th year of his title as the chief wrestler, he would wrestle with Yusuf from Deliorman.

The announcer (cazgır) introduced first Aliço and then Yusuf. Both wrestlers greeted the spectators and started with the warm-up session (*peşrev*). Aliço was as quick and agile as a young wrestler. Yusuf's warm-

---

[104] Mehmet Niyazi, *Zaman*.

up movements with his big hands were masterly and flashy. It was apparent from his movements that he was a competent wrestler.

The warm-up session was followed by the pull-down attacks (*elense*). Few wrestlers could survive Aliço's pull-down attacks. Seeing Yusuf stand firm against Aliço's attacks, the spectators were excited. They knew they were watching an enjoyable match. To show that he was not intimidated by Yusuf, Aliço was staying upright so that his rival might try to attack his lower parts and he could put him into his famous headlocks.

However, Yusuf was not making the move to get a hold of Aliço's pants. One hour had passed since the start of the wrestling and Yusuf was now responding to Aliço's pull-down attacks. The pull-down attacks Yusuf made with his big hands made Aliço realize that his rival was very strong. He couldn't understand why Yusuf wasn't taking advantage of the soft spots he was intentionally revealing.

He believed a lengthy match would be to this advantage as he could wrestle for hours. But realizing that Yusuf was not exhausted after about two hours of wrestling, Aliço changed his tactic and made a quick double takedown attack. In response, Yusuf swiftly turned back and fell prostrate. Crawling on his knees, Aliço pushed him down on his belly, not allowing him to stand up.

Yusuf made moves to get rid of Aliço's hold, but saw it was no avail. So he took a completely defensive position. After taking his rival under his full control, Aliço started to prepare for hobbling his rival. But at that moment, Yusuf escaped Yusuf's clutches and stood up and faced Aliço with an intimidating cry. Gaped by the strength and agility of Yusuf, everyone was encouraging both sides for a good match. Yusuf started to wrestle without falling down again.

The pace of the wrestling was not waning although hours had passed. It was hard to predict who will win. But the wrestling aficionados could sense that Yusuf was better conditioned. The old age of Aliço was starting to betray him. As the evening was drawing nearer, Aliço realized that his moves were no longer swift.

But Aliço was as much chivalrous as he was pitiless. He could be fair about everything. He was not feeling sorry. He had realized that Yusuf deserved the title. Now he could readily quit wrestling. He was sure the wrestler such as Adalı Halil and Yusuf would properly maintain the tradition. With these thoughts in his mind, he decided to be easier with his rival. Now, he wasn't being rough and pitiless with his attacks and moves.

Everyone wanted a wrestler who defended the title as the chief wrestler of Kırkpınar for 26 years to quit wrestling in an honorable way. Now, it was all the darker. In his old age, Aliço had wrestled all through the day like a young wrestler, showing the intricacies of the art. On the other hand, Yusuf proved to be a skillful wrestler.

At those who tried to put an end to the match with a draw, Aliço shouted: "This is Kırkpınar. The stage is set for valiant wrestlers. Here the match goes on until one beats the other. There are barrels of bitumen and kindling woods over there. Kindle them for light. A heated match shouldn't be interrupted. If this fledgling boy will beat me, let him do so. I will stop wrestling actively. This is the best chance for Yusuf to beat Aliço."

Hearing these words, Yusuf was overwhelmed with a torrent of emotions and rushed toward Aliço and took his hands and said: "You are the master of masters, top wrestler. Let us quit wrestling. You beat me with your words. All my strength is drained. I cannot hold you after what you said. If you want, you hold me and pin my back on the ground."

Aliço, too, was moved and about to cry: "This arena is yours. Seeing a wrestler like you emerge, I will not look back. Both the prize and the title are yours. Have them both. Enjoy them in the best way." And he declared Yusuf as the winner. Now, the chief wrestler was Yusuf...[105]

Now, let us think about this story. Let us compare the ambitions of people who try to beat their rival through all sorts of intrigues and tricks today with the very spirit of our ancestors in this story? Where do the people of our time stand in the face of the chivalry and humility our ancestors could exhibit even when they beat their rivals? History shows that how the values of our culture and civilization were cherished and gives us an enthusiasm for cherishing them once again.

In our story, Aliço knew that a true wrestler should be fair with his rivals and Yusuf showed humility even when he defeated a long time

---

[105] Eşref Şefik, *Tarihi Türk Güreşçileri* (Historic Turkish Wrestlers), p. 103.

champion. Like this story that shows what a real chivalry is, we have many lessons to learn from our glorious past to rediscover our values and power. It is an important task to delve into the archives and find these lessons for the sake of historical awareness.

QUESTIONS

1. Who are truly God-revering according to the Holy Qur'an?
   a. Those possessed of true knowledge
   b. The rich
   c. The administrators
   d. None

2. In a *hadith*, our Prophet says that the ink of the scholars will be weighed with ....? Which one of following phrases best fills the blank in this sentence?
   a. The sweat of the *mujahid*
   b. The blood of the martyrs
   c. The tears of the worshipers
   d. The tears of the mothers

3. To whom do Allah, angels, everything on earth and in the skies, and all creatures including the ants in their nests and the fish in the seas pray, as stated in a *hadith*?
   a. Indolent people
   b. Those who feed the poor
   c. The teachers who teach good deeds to the public
   d. The traders

4. Which of the phrases best filling in the blanks in the *hadith*, ".................... stretch their wings over the student who leaves home to acquire knowledge, and Allah facilitates the way to .... for him"?
   a. Parents – success   b. Birds – home
   c. The jinn – Hell   d. Angels – Paradise

5. Who acted as a student until his death as reported by his disciple Matar al-Warraq?
   a. Qatada   b. Tolstoy
   c. Emile Zola   d. Frederic Henry

6. Which Ottoman sultan took three mule-loads of books with him during a military campaign against Egypt?

   a. Sultan Mehmed the Conqueror

   b. Yavuz Sultan Selim

   c. Suleiman the Magnificent

   d. Bayezid II

7. How is the community of Companions whose sole purpose to acquire knowledge and attain Allah's pleasure by doing so called?

   a. Shuhada Uhud   b. Dar al-Nadwa

   c. Ashab al-Badr   d. Ashab al-Suffa

ANSWERS

	1. Why Should We Acquire Fine Morals?	2. Rights of Parents	3. Camaraderie and Friendship	4. Benevolence	5. Truthfulness, Honesty, Veracity and Keeping Promises	6. Etiquette and Manners	Appendix: The Importance of Reading
1	c	a	a	a	b	d	a
2	b	d	d	b	d	d	b
3	a	c	a	d	d	b	c
4	a	a	c	c	b	c	d
5	d	d	b	b	a	a	a
6	c		d	a	a	c	b
7	d		d	b	d	c	d
8	d		b	a	a	d	
9			a	d	c	a	
10			d	b	c	c	